MW00593706

How sweet your
words taste to me;
they are sweeter than honey.
Your commandments
give me understanding;
no wonder I hate
every false way of life.

Psalm 119:103-104 nlt

Introduction

The immediate reward of honey is its sweet taste. But honey also has incredible health benefits. Similarly, God's Word has both instant and lasting advantages. The wisdom found within its pages requires time spent searching and meditating. True understanding happens through prayer and an intimate relationship with God.

Be encouraged as you savor the Scriptures, devotions, and prayers in this devotional. God has shown immeasurable love and grace, and his undeserved kindness is revealed in his mercies that are new every morning. Taste the goodness of his lifegiving words that are both sweet and strong and be nourished by the richness of his wisdom and compassion.

JANUARY

Gracious words
are a honeycomb,
sweet to the soul
and healing to the bones.

PROVERBS 16:24 NIV

ABOVE ALL

Let all who take refuge in you rejoice;
let them sing joyful praises forever.
Spread your protection over them,
that all who love your name may be filled with joy.
PSALM 5:11 NLT

You are probably entering this New Year with new goals in mind. Whether they are physical, financial, or relational, this year is a fresh start for you to pursue good things. While you may already have all your goals in mind, it would be good to put this one at the top of your list: pursue Christ above all. Your relationship with him is the most important thing you can go after this year.

The Word tells us that when we take refuge in God, we rejoice. Those whose hearts are hidden in God are full of joyful praise. When we are loving the things of Christ, life is abundant, and peace filled. What could be better? It will likely require sacrifice of some things that we would normally otherwise pursue, and then also the denial of other desires. It will not be in vain. We should set our sights on the pursuit of God's goodness, and in this we will find our joy complete.

God, this New Year is yours, and my plans pale in comparison to those you have for me. Help me pursue you foremost, knowing that if a deep relationship with you is what I have at the end of this year, I have succeeded.

HIDDEN GEMS

I have hidden your word in my heart,
that I might not sin against you.
PSALM 119:11 NLT

Life is full, and during some seasons all you might have time for is a page from this devotional. May that page turn your thoughts to God as you chug your coffee. While you may be adopting the "something is better than nothing" mentality in more than one area of your life, your walk with God is one you don't want to shortchange.

Scripture is powerful, and it is particularly influential when you meditate on it throughout the day. Have you ever had a song stuck in your head? That's what you're aiming for here. Ponder on a verse in the morning. Repeat it to yourself as you get ready for your day. Review it over your lunch break. Savor it and ask yourself, "What does this tell me about God?" or "What does this tell me about how God sees me?" When the Word is in your mind, it impacts the way you live each day, and consequently your life.

Holy Spirit, help me give time to your Word, so my mind is ruled by it. Of all the things I could think about, I know your Word is the most important. It brings life to my days.

SUSTENANCE

Sustain me, my God, according to your promise,
and I will live; do not let my hopes be dashed.
PSALM 119:116 NIV

What keeps each of us going throughout our days? Could it be a midday nap, an afternoon cup of tea, or a walk that gets the blood flowing? Whatever the method of choice, all of us have things that help sustain us through our long days. Beyond the midday slump, our souls require sustaining, too, and whether we realize it or not we are constantly on the search for something that will fill us, satisfy our hungers, and give us a reason to wake up and go to workday after day.

God promises to sustain us, and his bearing up of our soul brings life and hope where other things fall short. We need to take account of the state of our hearts in this moment. What are we giving ourselves to in hope of satisfaction? What are we pursuing in anticipation of numbing our pain? Dear one, it is in Christ alone that our hopes will not be dashed. We can set aside all else and find our peace in him.

God, I repent of pursuing created things that give me energy for a short period of time. I know all too well that I will be disappointed in the end. Help me instead to seek you when I feel myself drifting toward false support.

BEAUTIFUL INHERITANCE

The LORD is my chosen portion and my cup;
you hold my lot.
The lines have fallen for me in pleasant places;
indeed, I have a beautiful inheritance.
PSALM 16:5-6 ESV

Perhaps you woke up this morning considering all the things that are not right in your life—your finances, your marriage, your job, your health. There are countless things in life that can be put in the category of "grievances," but today is a day for recognizing God's goodness.

Regardless of your circumstances today, you have been chosen by God to be a part of his family, and therefore you are blessed. You have a beautiful inheritance in Christ, and while the culmination of God's blessings has not yet arrived, the realization of his goodness starts today. Will you, like the wandering Israelites, demand relief from pain and insecurity, or will you choose Christ as your portion, the source of all you will ever need? His grace is sufficient (2 Corinthians 12:9), and his goodness pursues you (Psalm 23:6). May you draw peace from that knowledge.

Jesus, it is foolish of me to complain when I consider the many ways you have blessed me and given me the hope of a beautiful inheritance. Cause my heart to rest in contentment today.

TRULY GOOD

You are good and do only good;
teach me your decrees.
PSALM 119:68 NLT

Who among us would knowingly let ourselves be led by false teachers or deceivers claiming to have our best interests in mind? Every day we are up against the deceptions of this world, and many times we allow ourselves to be misled by that which looks good but actually plots to destroy us. Materialism, consumerism, and influencers who emphasize what feels good rather than obedience to Christ—they are all ploys of the enemy to wean our hearts from the source of all that is good.

How are we to combat these sweet deceptions except by steeping our minds in what is good and true? The entire book of Psalms tells us that God is good and only does good—shouldn't it be God we seek to learn from? Let's accept the challenge today to note what seemingly good things are being influential at a personal level. How do they compare to the truth of Scripture?

God, forgive me for allowing myself to be swayed by things that look and sound good but really are empty. These things, I know, will leave me aching. Help me to fill up on the truth of your Word so that I am not tempted to binge on lesser things.

VICTORY IN CHRIST

"For your sake we are killed all day long;
we were regarded as sheep to be slaughtered."
ROMANS 8:36-37 NASB

Chances are we are all under attack today. Regardless of our cognizance of the spiritual forces which seek to deter us from walking in God's path, they are real and present. Scripture tells us that we who belong to Christ are like sheep being led to the slaughter every day. In other words, we are constantly under attack due to our relationship with Jesus. Satan wants nothing more than to create doubt instead of trust, disassemble our relationships, and lead us to a false belief that it's best when we take the wheel.

We have the power when we realize this, though. The victory is ours when we are aware of the attack, we speak against our enemy, and we can then claim triumph over him in the name of Jesus. Today, remember that there is literally nothing that can separate you from the love of Jesus. Be aware of your enemy but walk in the victory that is yours through Christ.

Thank you, Holy Spirit, for the power that is mine to wage war against the enemy. Thank you for reminders of the battle that I face, but also of the victory that is mine because I am your child.

BOAST-WORTHY

"Those who wish to boast should boast in this alone: that they truly know me and understand that I am the LORD who demonstrates unfailing love and who brings justice and righteousness to the earth, and that I delight in these things. I, the LORD, have spoken!"

JEREMIAH 9:23-24 NLT

We're proud of our strengths. Whether it's our beauty, talent, or intelligence, we take pride in the things which we are good at. But better than anything that we possess on our own is the ability to know and understand the things of God. And what does God, who is all-powerful and all-knowing, desire that we boast in?

God, in his glorious humility, desires that the things we brag on are things that the world would find rather weak and dull. We can proudly profess the love that does not grow tired, the mercy extended to the undeserving, and the triumph in the right thing when the right thing is terribly difficult. Next time we feel the need to justify ourselves by sharing our own good qualities, let's remember the things Christ finds boast worthy.

God, you remind me that the things that the world finds pleasing mean nothing to you. May these things—love and mercy, justice and righteousness—be the same things I treasure and boast in.

COURAGE

LORD, you are my shield,
my wonderful God who gives me courage.
PSALM 3:3 NCV

As a child or young adult, courage might seem like something called upon for great, meaningful accomplishments like saving someone from drowning, perhaps. But as we grow older, we learn that courage is most necessary when life's pressures mount, struggle knocks on the door, or the burden of pain causes our shoulders to slump. It is not only in the life-altering moments of heroism when we need courage. We will call on it the mornings after a fight with our spouse, when our child uses words like knives, the day our job lets us go, or when depression creeps in.

On these days, it is vital to remember the source of our strength. It is imperative that we do not shut the door to block out the world without first turning our gaze heavenward. On these days we must lay hold of the courage that our wonderful God offers us. We can lift up our heads because our help is on the way even before we pray.

Jesus, life is sweet when I trust you. I know that regardless of my struggle you are with me, and you are the source of my courage and joy. Help me look to you today.

MADE RIGHTEOUS

As for me, by your abundant graciousness
I will enter your house,
at your holy temple I will bow in reverence for you.
PSALM 5:7 NASB

None of us is perfect; we all have our flaws and secret sins. It is easy to see the unrighteousness of those who lead wicked lives, who boast about evil, or take pleasure in wrongdoing. When we compare ourselves to those who are outwardly immoral, we tend to feel that we are doing a pretty good job. In reality, sin is sin, and no one is righteous in his own merit. But what grace has been extended to those of us who have trusted Jesus; because we are covered in the blood of Christ, the Father sees us as righteous and welcomes us as if we have done no wrong.

We each can thank Jesus for his abundant grace. We deserved death, but God in his mercy brought us into his house. Today, when we see the depravity of the world around and we are tempted to consider ourselves virtuous, remember that it is only by the sweet grace of Christ that we can draw near to God.

Oh Lord, you are so gracious. Thank you for covering me in righteousness when I deserved death. Let me live today with a thankful spirit.

TRUE LOVE

Let your unfailing love surround us, LORD,
for our hope is in you alone.
PSALM 33:22 NLT

Chick flicks and rom coms have long given us a definition of love which modern women so often cling to in their search for romance. Love is willing to chase us through the airport to stop our flight. Love will give up hopes and dreams in order to fulfill ours. Love will deny family relationships in order to pursue one true love. Rarely, if ever, do we see a display of love that goes beyond the initial attraction and pursuit.

This sets us up for misunderstanding real love, but it's time to set things straight. Real love is quieter but no less extraordinary. Real love is faithful. Real love continues to show up despite our inadequacies. Real love sees the best and the worst and chooses to accept both. Real love allows room for mistakes, growth, and setbacks; it always hopes for better. Real love is Christ.

Jesus, thank you for demonstrating true love—love that is unfailing, everlasting, always patient, and always hopeful. Forgive me for assuming that love is only loud and bold. Help me see the beauty in your quiet, faithful love.

Trustworthy

Everything he does is good and fair;
all his orders can be trusted.

Psalm 111:7 ncv

In today's world, maybe more than ever before, doubt
is everywhere. We suspect everyone and everything;
wariness always precedes believing the best of someone.
It is no surprise, then, that our view of God's Word and his
call to us as believers is also met with hesitation.

Yet Scripture could not be clearer about the
trustworthiness of God and his Word. Imagine knowing
someone who always did what was right and good,
brought comfort in the midst of trial, found the good in
every situation, and followed through on every single
promise. That is our God. He is completely good, and
his Word is entirely trustworthy. Is he asking you to do
something about which you have been uncertain? Has he
called you to action, but you've been doubtful that he'll
see you through? Hesitate no more, friend.

God, thank you that I can trust you completely. Forgive me
for doubting your Word. Help me learn to depend upon
your goodness to lead me through my days. Let me not
delay in obeying your commands.

GRACE IN EVERY SEASON

My soul clings to the dust;
give me life according to your word!
PSALM 119:25 ESV

Life can be heavy. For the Christ-follower, hard times are guaranteed (John 16:33). We have days when our souls feel dragged through the dust—when our lungs just can't seem to breathe in enough air. Those days, or weeks, or months can drag on until we have lost all hope. It is not easy to say or easy to hear, but it is vital to understand that those times are a form of grace.

When life is simple, pleasant, or straightforward we tend to think that it is our own capability which has caused things to level out for us. We forget that we are but a vapor and our entire existence is dependent on the Creator's mercy. But when the burdens begin to stack up, when our backs and hearts break under the pressure, it is then in that painful grace-filled season, that we remember who sustains us. If life is heavy today, cry out as the psalmist did for life according to his Word. He promises to strengthen us.

Oh Lord, thank you that every season of life is full of your grace. Give me strength for today as I trust in you.

GODLY LIFE

His divine power has given us everything we need for a godly life through our knowledge of him who called us by his own glory and goodness.

2 PETER 1:3 NIV

Perhaps you woke up this morning unprepared for the day. The kids slept poorly, your project's deadline got moved up, and the coffee maker wouldn't work. You want nothing more than to return to bed and hit the restart button. But life awaits. How will you respond? It is tempting to think that on those days God understands our angst and will surely tolerate a less-than-ideal attitude coming from us.

But we know better. Peter tells us that God's divine power has given us *everything* we need for living a godly life. This isn't just on the days when we get enough sleep and coffee but maybe specifically on the days when everything seems to go wrong. By his goodness we have been called, not to get by with our teeth clenched and our hearts set on the end of this awful day. Instead, we have been called to live a life of humility, patience, self-sacrifice, and joy. This is how Jesus lived. Take a moment and ask for God's grace to live a godly life today.

God, help me today to choose joy. You have given me all I need, not just to endure this day but to make it sweet and beneficial. May it be so according to your grace.

REFUGE

Taste and see that the Lord is good.
Oh, the joys of those who take refuge in him!
PSALM 34:8 NLT

What do you take refuge in? We all have something. Maybe for you it is a good workout to burn away the day's stress, or the time at night when the kids are finally in bed, or perhaps it is the accolades you receive on social media. A refuge is a safe place—a place where we run and hide from the troubles of our lives. But what happens when the very thing we count on for our safe place is unavailable to us?

Scripture tells us to taste and see—to experience with our senses and with our whole being—that the Lord is good. He is a good place to hide ourselves when things are getting tough. His refuge offers peace for our minds and joy for our hearts. It is not dependent on things going a certain way; it cannot be taken from us when the day takes unexpected turns. We need to check our hearts today and make sure we are hiding ourselves in the certainty of Christ.

God, I admit that I rely on created things to relieve my stress and bring me joy. I know that true and lasting joy is only found in you. Help me take hold of that today.

ALWAYS FAITHFUL

"The LORD, the LORD, a God merciful and gracious, slow to anger, and abounding in steadfast love and faithfulness, keeping steadfast love for thousands, forgiving iniquity and transgression and sin."

EXODUS 34:6-7 ESV

Close your eyes for a moment and think back on the last month of your life. Consider the hard days and the good days and think about them in light of God's faithfulness. What stands out to you? Does his faithfulness make itself known in extraordinary and loud ways, much like the parting of the Red Sea? Or does it barely come through, like a light that seeps out through a crack in the door?

God's faithfulness, we are told, is abounding. That doesn't always mean it's flashy and audacious. Sometimes it is the quiet but sustaining force that carries us through a dark season. We might not even be aware of it until after the fact. But the reality is that we are never without it. Thank you, God for your abounding, ever-present faithfulness in our lives.

Lord, thank you for the ways you have proven yourself faithful in my life. Forgive me for the times that I fail to recognize it. Help me be more aware of the ways you extend your faithfulness and love to me.

FREEDOM

I will live in freedom,
because I want to follow your orders.
PSALM 119:45 NCV

As a young adult, Heather couldn't wait for the day when she lived on her own and made her own rules. She longed for freedom to make plans and follow her own dreams. When she was twenty-two years old, she was finally out on her own and tasting the freedom she had yearned for. It wasn't long, however, before she realized that life on her own didn't hold the fulfillment that she had assumed it would. Her actions held consequences, and she began to understand that it wasn't freedom from rules or authority that she needed.

Heather began to appreciate Scripture which gives guidelines for how life works best. She saw wisdom in God's instructions—how they provided protection, gave advice for tough situations, and spoke of God's mercy that always attended her even in her mistakes. Freedom, she found, was not in independence and making her own rules; it was found in bowing to Christ and discovering the peaceful sovereignty by which her life was ruled.

God, sometimes I wish to do things my own way. Thank you for the reminder that freedom is found in my obedience to your Word which speaks of your desire for my best life.

FEAST FOR THE SOUL

You satisfy me more than the richest feast.
I will praise you with songs of joy.
PSALM 63:5 NLT

It's amazing to have a satisfying meal after a long day of hard work. Our bodies were made for nourishment, and they work best when they are regularly fed with good, nutrient-rich food. Similarly, our souls were not made to fast for extended periods of time; we need regular nourishment from the source of life—Jesus. Just like a feast at the richest of celebrations which offers all the good things we could want to eat, Jesus eases the pangs of hunger that our souls experience living in this world.

We are constantly looking for ways to fulfill our longing for more, but the created world was never meant to satiate our thirst. What things are you pursuing to fill you? Make sure you are giving your soul regular nourishment by spending time in the Word and in prayer with your heavenly Father. You will be satisfied.

Jesus, thank you for satisfying my longings with your presence and your joy. Forgive me for seeking other things to fill the void in my heart and help me pursue you alone.

WORTH LOOKING AT

Turn my eyes from looking at worthless things;
and give me life in your ways.
PSALM 119:37 ESV

God made us to appreciate art in many forms—paintings, cinematography, street art, photography. It's a privilege to enjoy beautiful things that give us pleasure. But with the sinful nature which we are all born into, it is all too easy for appreciation to develop into an obsession, or to allow our eyes to enjoy things that will tempt us into sin.

Scripture tells us to ask for help in turning our eyes from worthless things; God knew that our tendency would be to allow ourselves to dwell on things that—while maybe not inherently bad—could become too important and take away from seeing and seeking good things. How much time do you give to the best thing—God's Word? Check your heart and your time today, and make sure you are meditating on what will serve your heart well.

God, I need help in turning my eyes away from things that do not encourage my relationship with you. Forgive me and help me dwell on things that are pure and lovely.

SHAMELESS

I will speak of your statutes before kings
and will not be put to shame.
PSALM 119:46 NIV

Lily often found herself speaking quietly when she was
publicly discussing spiritual matters with her friends or
her children. What if someone heard and was offended,
or called her out for being judgmental and contradicted
her beliefs? What if she didn't know how to respond?
The more she studied the Scriptures, the more confident
Lily felt in speaking boldly about Christ. She did not care
if she were ridiculed, and she hoped that she would be
overheard, and then asked about her beliefs. The Spirit
lived in her and empowered her to share the truth.

The modern world makes us afraid of speaking about
Christ, but why fear? We are the ones with the truth! Ask
the Spirit to embolden you to speak confidently and
without shame whenever you have the opportunity to
share the sweetness of knowing Christ.

God, my natural inclination is to keep quiet about you,
but you are the one whom I am absolutely unashamed of
knowing! Give me courage to share boldly, knowing that I
will not be put to shame for speaking the truth.

WELCOMED HOME

Do not turn away from me.
Do not turn your servant away in anger;
you have helped me.
Do not push me away or leave me alone,
God, my Savior.
PSALM 27:9 NCV

Have you ever experienced the silent treatment? Angry friends or loved ones can push us away when we have hurt them, refusing to speak to us when we desperately want connection and reconciliation. Perhaps you've been the one to refuse a restored relationship at times in your life. When we have sinned against God it is natural to think that he will respond with the same anger that we have received in our lives from others. We're expecting to be pushed away and received with stony silence when we plea for reconciliation.

But what mercy is ours when we approach his throne of grace! Instead of anger, we find love. Instead of God shunning us, we find his open arms. Instead of abandoning our friendship, we find him rejoicing to restore our relationship. God's mercy is just waiting for us to return. We need to not delay.

Oh God, how merciful and good you are! Thank you for not tiring of welcoming me back. Help me walk in righteousness today and every day.

HURRYING BACK TO GOD

I thought about my life,
and I decided to follow your rules.
I hurried and did not wait
to obey your commands.
PSALM 119:59-60 NCV

Imagine you went hiking in the Rocky Mountains. The path was winding and beautiful, and you were overcome with wonder as you traversed the trail. But suddenly you realized you were no longer on the path. Somewhere along the way you must have missed a turn, and now you must be lost. You certainly would not hesitate in turning back in order to find the trail. You wouldn't say to yourself, "I've come this far, I'll just go a little farther before turning around."

Now think about your spiritual life. When you realize you are not walking in righteousness, how quickly do you turn back to the Lord? Oftentimes shame, pride, or your sinful desires keep you from repenting and hurrying back to God. But what dangers lie in wait for you when you do not turn in haste back from your sin! Just as darkness can fall and prevent you from getting to safety on a mountain trail, you can also put yourself in a dangerous place when you hesitate to come back to God.

God, forgive me for hesitating to repent and return to your ways. I know that you will not meet me with a heavy hand; thank you for your mercy.

GOVERNED BY GOODNESS

The LORD is good to everyone.
He showers compassion on all his creation.
PSALM 145:9 NLT

What are the implications of God's divine attributes in your life today? You might have a basic understanding of God's goodness, but does it affect the way you live? God's nature causes him to be good to all mankind. He is compassionate, kind, and merciful (Isaiah 30:18). He is patient and does not want anyone to perish; he is hoping for all to repent (2 Peter 3:9). So how does this knowledge change the way you live today?

Hopefully, the awareness of God's goodness will cause a spirit of humility to rise up in you; hopefully it inspires you to extend the same goodness to others that you have received yourself. It may allow you to see the body of Christ as well as those whose hearts are far from God with the same level of compassion—breathing out kindness to those who love you as well as those who persecute you. It will hopefully cause you to repent from sin and return to God with joy, being confident that he will receive you back as if you had never sinned.

Oh God, cause your goodness to change me from the inside out. May I live, not with knowledge alone, but with a heart governed by your goodness.

THE SOURCE OF JOY

Those who sing as well as those
who play the flutes will say,
"All my springs of joy are in you."
PSALM 87:7 NASB

Any one of us could tell the next person how life is a series of ups and downs. The highest highs and the lowest lows weave together to form the messy tapestry of life. As followers of Christ, it is important that we see each moment—wonderful or tragic—as an opportunity to praise God for being our source of joy. Today, are you embracing where Christ has you, allowing him to shape your character and your story according to his will? Or are you waiting for things to change, to improve, to be the green grass of a happy life that someone else already seems to have?

Today, I challenge you to consider how you are viewing your life, and ask yourself, "Am I connected to the source of my joy?" Allow yourself to repent of longing for an earthly utopia and embrace your present situation. Embrace the fact that Jesus is enough for you even when nothing else is.

Jesus, if you are all I have, I have it all. Thank you for being my source of joy in all seasons of my life. You are sufficient for my every need.

RIGHTS VERSUS PROMISES

Let us hold fast the confession of our hope without wavering, for he who promised is faithful.
HEBREWS 10:23 ESV

Gigi was peeved. The restful night of sleep she longed for had once again evaded her for no apparent reason. Here she was serving in ministry, sacrificing herself in order to bring others into the family of faith, and she couldn't even get a full night's sleep. She was annoyed with God—where were his blessings? She sulked through her day, but the Spirit wouldn't let her get away with her complaining. She finally realized that she was clinging to good sleep as if it were something she was entitled to. She had turned it into a right, something which had never been promised.

In that moment she repented and began to count the things of God which are promised to her: the love of God that cannot be removed (Romans 8:38-39), abundant life—with or without good sleep (John 10:10); the care of the Father (1 Peter 5:7), a purpose in life which will be fulfilled according to his will (Ephesians 2:10), and that all of God's promises to his people are a resounding, "Yes!" in Christ (2 Corinthians 1:20). What things are you holding fast to that were never promised?

God, I know I can trust your promises because you are faithful. Help me cling to them instead of clinging to the things I have contrived an entitlement to.

FOUNDATION OF UNDERSTANDING

Before the mountains were born
and before you created the earth and the world,
you are God.
You have always been, and you will always be.

PSALM 90:2 NCV

What have you based your heart's understanding of God upon? How you perceive God will impact you—for better or worse—and the way you live your life. We know what God is like because of what Scripture says, because of the Spirit living in us, and because of the body of Christ who helps us grasp his character. But what is your understanding of God really based upon?

It is all too easy to comprehend God through the lens of our human experience, allowing that lens to define God for us. This might cause us to see him as someone who withholds good from us, or who loves us based on what we do, or who is untrustworthy. All of these notions are false according to Scripture and will lead us to an understanding of God that is not worthy of him. Today, check the foundation for your comprehension of God.

God, forgive me for creating in my mind a god that is not based upon the truth of your Word. Instead, I have based my faith upon my limited human experiences. Help me to know you rightly.

SOVEREIGN GOODNESS

We know that God causes all things to work together
for good to those who love God, to those who are called
according to his purpose.

ROMANS 8:28 NASB

Life is full of conflict. From birth, our stories are built on
overcoming conflict or bending and breaking as a result of
it. Perhaps today you find yourself in a battle and you are
struggling to perceive the blessing that will come from it.
But as believers we must have faith that there is no battle
we will face which will not produce some good.

Do you believe strongly in the sovereignty and goodness
of God? Do you rise to the occasion when conflict occurs,
waiting with anticipation for how God will show his
goodness? Or do you avoid trouble at all costs and then
panic when it finds you? Here is something to remember:
if you belong to God, you cannot lose. Regardless of your
battle, you are sure to win if you are on God's side.

God, thank you that no temptation has seized me except
that which is common to man (1 Corinthians 10:13). You
knew my battles before you created everything, and you
knew the blessings that would arise from them according
to your sovereign goodness. Help me trust that today.

WEAKNESS OF RESOLVE

The one who calls you is faithful,
and he will do it.
1 THESSALONIANS 5:24 NIV

We have certainly all resolved to make things happen in our lives. Maybe for you it is a resolve to create a life that is different than the one you had growing up. Perhaps it is to fit into a certain clothing size, or to reach the top of your company. Determination can be a noble trait, but there are certain things that we will never attain through resolve alone. Holiness is one of those. We cannot will away our sinful nature, nor determine that we will reach perfection. It is only through the faithful work of the Holy Spirit in our lives and our willingness to hear and obey that we will ever reach sanctification (Philippians 2:13).

What are you determined to see happen in your own life? If you have been trying in your own willpower to please God, or to overcome a recurring sin, or maybe to see freedom from addiction you will only find yourself worn out, defeated, and ready to give up. Cry out to your faithful God; he will help you.

God, thank you that you have not left me on my own to reach holiness. You are faithful and I need your help.

CHAOS

People may make plans in their minds,
but the LORD decides what they will do.
PROVERBS 16:9 NCV

All we want in life is smooth sailing with ourselves in the pilot seat and Jesus as co-pilot. "We'll go together, Lord, but I'll make the calls." Perhaps we don't say that out loud or even consciously think it, but honestly—sometimes we wish Jesus would stop changing or influencing our own strategies.

Here's the thing, though. Jesus loves us too much to let us invest in plans which will benefit our egotistical, individualistic, sinful selves. That might sound harsh but bear with me. Jesus allows chaos in our lives to deter us from self-infatuation, creating plans and reaching goals that will cause us to think "I did this." He knows that dependence on him will only come if we are shaken out of the daydream that we can accomplish things on our own. It is his great love and mercy that swipes the rug out from under our feet. The next time everything starts breaking down, thank Jesus for piloting us.

Jesus, I know it is your mercy that causes me to lose control of so many situations. Thank you for being on the throne, sovereignly managing all the things in my life that I thought I could handle on my own.

FAITHFUL JOY

We do this by keeping our eyes on Jesus, the champion who initiates and perfects our faith. Because of the joy awaiting him, he endured the cross, disregarding its shame. Now he is seated in the place of honor beside God's throne.

HEBREWS 12:2 NLT

Jesus knew what it meant to suffer in life. In all the things he faced throughout his ministry leading to his death on the cross, he was faithful. Life for him, as it is for all of us, was not rainbows and butterflies; it was a challenge. It was dealing with people who scorned him and didn't believe in his goodness. In the end, they had him killed for being the best.

In all of this, Jesus did not lose sight of the promise the Father gave him: his sheep that would be rescued as a result of his life and death. He showed us how to live a life of steadfastness and joy in the midst of difficulty. We should spend some time today praying this prayer for our own lives today.

God, I desire joy and steadfastness. I desire to not be dragged along by life but to stand tall, strong, and joyful in the midst of monotony, sleeplessness, grey days, and a demanding job. I do not want to live a defeated life. Direct my heart to the steadfastness of Christ and teach me to count it all joy.

EVER TRUE

Your kingdom is an everlasting kingdom,
and your dominion endures throughout all generations.
The LORD is faithful in all his words
and kind in all his works.

PSALM 145:13 ESV

That fact that God is faithful rests entirely on his immutability. If God cannot change, then the concept of his faithfulness is completely secure and to be trusted entirely. If God cannot change, then every promise he has made is sure to stand. If God cannot change, we can live with the peaceful knowledge that he will never remove his love from us. If God cannot change, then we know that his kindness will continue to be extended to those who love God and walk in righteousness.

God is ever true to himself and to his Word. This ought to encourage our hearts today in the confidence of God's Word. Very little in this world is true, even when we are led to believe it is. But Scripture *is* true! Let's fill our hearts and minds with truth today, so that we are ready to discern the lies of the enemy and to stand firm in the knowledge of God's perfect faithfulness.

Lord, what comfort it brings my heart knowing that no promise you have ever made will fail. I can trust your Word completely and find confidence in arming myself with it as I face the spiritual forces of darkness.

SATISFIED BY THE SACRED

Because I am righteous, I will see you.
When I awake, I will see you face to face and be satisfied.
PSALM 17:15 NLT

We are created to yearn for the Savior, the one who fills
the void in our souls and stops the ache in our hearts. All
of human life is spent attempting to fill the emptiness
within, and it doesn't stop once we have found Jesus.
Unfortunately, our hearts are still prone to seek fulfillment
in other things, and it is a constant battle to find ourselves
satisfied in Christ.

We can tell what things we are looking to fill us by asking
the question, "What is sacred to me?" When we find it
difficult to give these things up, then we know that we are
not finding our satisfaction in Jesus. It's often the case that
too many other things are clouding our viewpoints. "Likes"
on social media, our child's appropriate behavior, dressing
well, or the need to have nice possessions may be some
of our "sacred" things. When we begin to give these up,
we find that we can actually see Jesus. And when we see
Jesus, nothing else will meet the standard.

God, forgive me for clouding my view of you with created
things. I know they will never truly fill me. Help me be
willing to set aside these things that I have made sacred so
that I can seek the one truly sacred purpose.

FEBRUARY

As for God,
His way is blameless;
The word of the LORD is refined;
He is a shield to all
who take refuge in Him.

PSALM 18:30 NASB

GRACED TO BE GRACIOUS

May God be gracious to us and bless us
and make his face to shine upon us,
that your way may be known on earth,
your saving power among all nations.

PSALM 67:1-2 ESV

God's grace abounds to those of us who belong to him. The manifestation of his grace in our lives is not just so we can be called his favored ones but so his salvation can be shown to the world. It is easy to accept his blessing, but it can be harder to accept his call to bless others. If we truly believe that God has graced us, then we will become gracious to the people God puts in our lives.

Is that reflected in your life today? Are you sitting pretty on the blessings of God but neglecting to ask him how you can now be a blessing by extending his grace to those around you? Whether it is toward your spouse, coworkers, children, neighbors, or even strangers, ask the Lord what it means to give grace as you have received. Do not allow yourself to know his blessings without also blessing the world around you— "that your way may be known on earth, your saving power among all nations."

God, thank you for choosing me to be a recipient of your grace. Let me not settle comfortably into your favor but let me be moved into action so I can show those around me the blessing of knowing Christ.

CONDEMNATION FOR JOY

Have mercy on me, O God,
according to your steadfast love;
according to your abundant mercy
blot out my transgressions.
Wash me thoroughly from my iniquity,
and cleanse me from my sin!

PSALM 51:1-2 ESV

Do you ever fall into the trap of feeling condemned for your sin? For those of us who have received salvation, condemnation is only a temptation used by our enemy, the devil. We know that there is no condemnation for those who are in Christ Jesus (Romans 8:1)!

It is necessary that we recognize when we rebel against God so we can receive mercy, but God desires that we live with joy for the salvation he has bought us (v.12). It's from Satan if we spend our days with hearts that are heavy under the burden of our sin or with guilt that shadows our good moments with God. If Satan is tempting you to dwell in guilt, take hold of the mercy offered to you by Christ, and let joy once again rule your heart.

I am undeserving of your forgiveness but so thankful that you have cleansed me. Help me live with a heart open to your mercy and joy, refusing the burden of condemnation.

Too Good Not to Share

They will burst forth in speaking
of your abundant goodness,
and will shout joyfully of your righteousness.

Psalm 145:7 NASB

Here's a challenge for you today: give your personal account of God's goodness in your life to someone near you. Scripture tells us to declare God's goodness and to sing of his righteousness. Have you done that lately? It is all too easy to fall into the rut of trudging through the monotony of daily life without taking time to acknowledge God's goodness in our ordinary days.

What does his goodness look like for you today? Did you get some quiet time before the kids woke up? Was there a day of sunshine after some stormy weather? Did you have an answer to prayer lately? Did you get to spend some time with an encouraging friend? Signs of God's goodness surrounds daily life; are you open to seeing it and declaring it? Do not let this day go by without taking the opportunity to burst forth in speaking about God's abundant goodness, just as the psalmist wrote.

Jesus, your goodness is worth sharing with others. Forgive me for getting so caught up in my day-to-day life that I have not taken the time to acknowledge and praise you for your blessings and abundant goodness. Help me see where you are declaring your love for me today.

DELIVERED NOT REMOVED

He is my loving God and my fortress,
my stronghold and my deliverer,
my shield, in whom I take refuge,
who subdues peoples under me.
PSALM 144:2 NIV

Gemma stayed home with her three young children. Her days were long, exhausting, and filled to the brim with arguments, discipline, and the constant feeling that she was losing control. She loved her children, but these young years began to feel more frustrating than enjoyable. She longed for deliverance to a more peaceful occupation than staying home with kids. It was disappointing the way it was turning out to be.

When she read about God being a fortress and deliverer, she initially thought that this would be true for her if she found a nanny. But then God revealed that being her fortress didn't necessarily mean taking her out of the battle. It meant finding a place of peace in God inside the disarray of home life. Gemma only needed to ensure that she was making a way to enter God's presence daily so she would be ready for the challenges ahead.

God, so often I expect that being rescued means finding relief from the challenges I face. I know that you are present always and that I can find security in you in the middle of the storm.

Unfailing Love

Your unfailing love is better than life itself;
how I praise you!
PSALM 63:3 NLT

Think about this for a moment: God's love for us is unfailing. It's hard to grasp since our minds are held to the confines of our flawed human understanding and experiences. Never in our lives have we truly encountered unfailing love from a person. Human love waxes and wanes; it shuts down when it's hurt; it withholds itself when it doesn't feel safe. As much as we may love another person or be loved by them, that love is imperfect.

Contrast this to the Lord's love for us. His love never wavers even when he is rejected. He gives all of himself every day when we are giving ourselves to other loves. He doesn't close off when we have pushed him away. He doesn't pursue another love when we are distracted. He always, infinitely, perfectly loves each of us. We need to let go of lesser things and open our hearts to that love today! Give praise to him for his love which is better than any other thing we could pursue.

God, thank you for pursuing me even when I am seeking other things. Your love goes so far beyond anything I can comprehend but help me grasp the depth of your love for me.

CALLED AND KEPT

I keep trying to reach the goal and get the prize for which
God called me through Christ to the life above.
PHILIPPIANS 3:14 NCV

What is something that you know God has called you to
that you have been struggling to fulfill lately? It could be a
job, a friend to minister to, or even regular time in the Word.
List out the reasons for your struggle. This may be more
challenging than you anticipated because you don't feel
equipped, you lack resources, or maybe you are worn out.

It is natural to come up against obstacles when we are
fulfilling the Lord's calling in our lives, and we should
even expect it! But if it is truly God who has called you
to this particular thing, then you know that he has set
your feet upon this path, and nothing can stop him from
accomplishing it! "He who calls you is faithful; he will
surely do it" (1 Thessalonians 5:24). *He* will do it. It has less
to do with your abilities and more with his faithfulness in
you. Ask him to empower and embolden you to carry on
with his calling in your life.

Lord, thank you that your calling does not depend on me
to accomplish it. You are faithful and trustworthy, and I
press on by the power of your Spirit to obtain the prize for
which you have called me.

Treasuring the Word

I have chosen the way of truth;
your judgments I have laid before me.
PSALM 119:30 NKJV

In order to treasure God's Word, there are two things that the believer must do: first, remove things in daily life that have been given higher value than the Word; second, put the Bible in the way. Let's elaborate. First, identify the things in life that have been made more important than God's Word. These can be identified by the use of time: clarify what the things are that regularly have priority over time in the Word. Once these distractions have been identified, remove them. Scripture says that if your eye causes you to stumble, gouge it out (Matthew 18:9). In other words, treat anything that gets in the way of time spent building a relationship with Christ like the enemy.

Now it will be easier to accomplish the second step: put the Word in the way. Write Scripture verses on cards and put them in the car, on the fridge, in the bathroom. Keep the Bible close at hand. Reach for it first in the morning instead of looking at the phone. In order to learn to treasure the Word, it has to be treated as the most important thing in life.

God, I am guilty of treasuring other things over your Word. I have chosen the way of truth but have not treasured your Word in my heart. Forgive me and help me!

RESTORATION

After you have suffered a little while, the God of all grace,
who has called you to his eternal glory in Christ, will
himself restore, confirm, strengthen, and establish you.
1 PETER 5:10 ESV

There is something about knowing that God himself will
restore us that makes suffering a little more bearable.
Imagine God walking along beside us, going with us
through the difficulties, and then when the time is right,
personally pulling us out of the deep waters. God doesn't
leave the work to someone else; he is intimately involved
in the process.

Whatever we are facing today, we need those moments
to acknowledge God's presence. He is not unaware of our
pain; he is walking with us and is prepared to restore us to
fullness of life in him by his grace. Eternal glory with Christ
is coming—for now, he is going along this journey with us.

Jesus, thank you for promising to personally restore,
confirm, strengthen, and establish me. My pains are not
mine to bear alone (Psalm 56:8), and my restoration comes
from the God of the universe. Thank you for knowing me
so intimately.

WAITING

Wait patiently for the LORD.
Be brave and courageous.
Yes, wait patiently for the LORD.
PSALM 27:14 NLT

Waiting is no one's favorite pastime. Waiting causes us to collide with our lack of patience. It goes against our natural desire to get what we want when we want it, and it shows us our lack of control over our own lives. While we can't usually change our circumstances to make the waiting period shorter, we can keep seeking the Lord while we wait.

Are you in a season of waiting? It can be challenging to wake up every day still lacking what you desire. But you will never be disappointed if you continue to go to God day after day while you wait for the fulfillment of your dream. Waiting is never the only thing to do for the believer. Wake up each morning and act upon your knowledge of God's grace for you because you belong to him. Wake up and praise him for his goodness to you today. Wake up and seek his heart for the people around you. You will not be disappointed.

Lord, thank you that while I wait, I have hope for the promise of good things. Help me seek you and not get so caught up in waiting for what's to come that I miss the gifts of today.

GRACE BETWEEN GRIEF

Surely goodness and mercy shall follow me
all the days of my life,
and I shall dwell in the house of the LORD forever.
PSALM 23:6 ESV

What grace can you find in your day today? Some days everything seems to go wrong all at once; your son breaks his finger, your car gets a flat on the way to the doctor, and you didn't get the promotion you were hoping for. Life has a way of storing up all its troubles, so they tumble down all at once. The sin nature wants to be consumed by it all.

We do not have to be consumed by all the bad news, though. When a torrent of troubles hits all at once, we can find grace woven between the griefs. What good things can we see and praise God for when life is throwing us curveballs? We are guaranteed to rise above the fog of despair that tends to settle on these hard days if we keep our gaze focused on the grace God promises. It follows us all the way through life. Psalm 23 is a beautiful song about God's amazing promise to us.

Lord, you truly are good to me, even when everything seems to be going wrong. Let me not be consumed by trouble, but instead help me change my perspective to see the grace that is surely in each situation.

No More Striving

"Their sins and lawless acts
I will remember no more."
And where these have been forgiven,
sacrifice for sin is no longer necessary.

Hebrews 10:17-18 NIV

Do you live your life as if you have been forgiven? Or is your life marked by striving for perfection, always paying penance for your sins? Friend, be reminded today that you have already been made perfect; no amount of striving to reach perfection and holiness will succeed because the holiness of Christ already rests in you. You do not need to pay penance for your sin—punishing yourself for your failure and trying to get right with God on your own is actually wrong in the sight of God. It has already been done for you!

The work to pay for your sins is complete. You can draw near to God in confidence, knowing that he doesn't see your mistakes anymore; all God sees is your righteousness in Christ Jesus. So, dear one, you should press onward into him in the full assurance of God's faithfulness, knowing that you are already accepted by him.

Oh Lord, how gracious you are to cover me in the holiness of Christ. Help me rest in the knowledge of my acceptance into your family, not by anything I have done, but only by your amazing grace.

NO SHAME IN RESTORATION

Instead of your shame you will have a double portion, and instead of humiliation they will shout for joy over their portion. Therefore they will possess a double portion in their land, everlasting joy will be theirs.

ISAIAH 61:7 NASB

It can be hard to see others further along in their journey with Christ, knowing that they have conquered sins that you still deal with daily. You might be asking the Lord, "When will it be my turn? When will I be free of these struggles?" Perhaps you feel ashamed, afraid that others will see you as less than, as someone who still has so far to go in their journey with Christ.

Satan wants you to feel shame over your struggles, but I want to reassure you that if the Lord is doing a work in your life, there is no shame in that. There is no shame in the Lord bringing restoration, even if it is taking longer than you had hoped. God has called you out of darkness into his marvelous light, and you are no longer enslaved as you once were. Do not compare your journey to someone else's; God will yet take your shame and replace it with joy over your inheritance!

God, let your joy rest upon me. Give me a full understanding of your tender love and encourage me as I walk toward restoration. Let me not be ashamed of the work you are doing in my life!

GRACIOUS OPPOSITION

For no one is cast off
by the Lord forever.
Though he brings grief, he will show compassion,
so great is his unfailing love.
LAMENTATIONS 3:31-32 NIV

Have you felt it—God's opposition to something in your life? It comes in many forms: sometimes it's gentle like a word from a trusted friend; other times it's aggressive like fire when you were hoping for cool water. It may feel harsh or unwarranted, but really, it is borne out of his love for you. God is so gracious that he will oppose you when you are going against his will; it is for your own good. He is after your heart and will take nothing less.

Perhaps you have been justifying something—a relationship, an addiction, or maybe a complaining spirit. God is too gracious to let you continue on that path. In his love for you he will make the storm tempestuous. Do not ignore his megaphone—wake up! Your pain may very well be a sign that something in your life needs to change. Check your heart today to be sure that you are walking uprightly.

Lord, I am thankful that you love me too much to allow me to pursue things that are not good for me. Help me be sensitive to your Spirit so I can quickly confess and return to you when I am not walking in righteousness.

PRACTICE PRACTICE PRACTICE

> This has been my practice:
> I obey your precepts.
> PSALM 119:56 NIV

We've surely all seen the effects of practice in our lives. Practice an instrument and there is success in the band competition. Practice a second language and we can speak it years afterwards. Practice concepts from high school algebra, and years later it will still be there to use in real life problems. But failure to practice means difficulty when it's time to try to pick it up again. "Use it or lose it," as they say.

This idea can apply to our relationships with Jesus too. Delighting ourselves in the Lord is not something that we will remember how to do if we have spent months filling our thoughts and spending our time on things other than him. Pursue the world and when we try to find our satisfaction in Christ again, we will struggle. But if we consistently practice, taking time every day to set our hearts and minds on Jesus, we will find a satisfied spirit dwelling within our souls.

Lord, help me be consistent in giving my heart to you. Spending time in your Word and in prayer will not leave me disappointed.

VALUE

Your teachings are worth more to me
than thousands of pieces of gold and silver.
PSALM 119:72 NCV

For most of us, speaking Psalm 119:72 to the Lord truthfully and with conviction would probably cause us to be hesitant. This is a big statement, and if we look honestly at our lives, the verse will probably not reflect our lives wholeheartedly.

Our pursuits show what we value if we take an honest look at life right now. For many of us, we would probably have to say that a version of the American Dream is governing our lives. We want, maybe not the very best, but good things, nice things, easy living, and safety. We want financial security, to provide for our families, and to not live in fear of ending up out on the streets. While these things are all worthy pursuits, if they are things we value most in life, we will find ourselves compromising the gospel in order to achieve stability. In that case, we would find Matthew's warning to be true for us: "It is worthless to have the whole world if they lose their souls" (Matthew 16:26).

Lord, help me give your Word its proper worth in my life. Let me not compromise but keep you first.

DOUBTING GOD'S GOODNESS

Surely God is good to Israel,
to those who are pure in heart.
PSALM 73:1 NIV

Psalm 73 speaks of one of God's own who was thinking foolishly and did not understand why the Lord allowed certain good things to happen to the wicked while he himself suffered for living righteously. He became embittered toward God because of it. It was not until he entered God's sanctuary that he "understood their final destiny" (v.17). And even though he had been foolish and doubtful of God, he went on to speak about the mercy of God which would remain with him, counseling him, and giving him honor.

How often have we acted this same way? We see people walking in wickedness, yet succeeding in life, at least in a worldly way, and we question the goodness and sovereignty of God. Do we forget that our God is a God of justice, and that the "Lord watches over the way of the righteous, but the way of the wicked leads to ruin" (Psalm 1:6)? Despite this our Lord continues to receive us back to him with open arms, regardless of our doubts.

Lord, you are so merciful. Forgive me for doubting your goodness, your sovereignty, and your justice. Thank you for dealing kindly with me and helping me to trust you.

FAVOR

I sought your favor with all my heart;
be gracious to me according to your word.
PSALM 119:58 NASB

Perhaps being popular isn't your thing, but you can probably admit to wanting to be found pleasing to others. Scripture says that Jesus, as a young man, grew in favor with God and people (Luke 2:52), so we know it's not a bad thing to be pleasing to others.

However, it is good practice to regularly ask yourself whose favor you are seeking. Are you seeking the approval of man, hoping to be admired and honored in your workplace, with family, or by friends? Are you spending your time doing things that you know will cause you to be seen in a good light so that you can fit in or be considered worthy of a certain group of people? Or can you genuinely say that you are pursuing the favor of the Lord with all your heart, looking to grow in righteousness and not concerning yourself with how the world views you? Once in a while, it is worthwhile to check the condition of the heart.

God, forgive me for looking to improve the way people see me, while failing to seek your favor and grow in righteousness. Help me to go after you first.

A HEART OF MERCY

You, O LORD, are a God merciful and gracious,
slow to anger and abounding
in steadfast love and faithfulness.

PSALM 86:15 ESV

Riley was struggling with her roommate. Their habits, preferences, and values were growing markedly different. It took all of Riley's willpower to treat her roommate with basic respect. She knew that circumstances made it impossible to find a new roommate at the moment, but something had to change. She thought of how Jesus responded to people who mistrusted and mistreated him. He was humble, kind, and acted in truth regardless of their actions toward him.

Riley came to believe that God had given her an opportunity to love her roommate despite their differences, for as long as they were together. She prayed for God's compassion to fill her heart, that she would show mercy instead of condemnation, and have eyes to see her friend with unaffected love just as Jesus saw her. Perhaps there is someone in your life whom you need to see with the eyes of Jesus. Ask him to give you a heart of compassion for that person.

Jesus, thank you for seeing me with love and mercy, even in my mistakes. Help me show that same kind of love to the people in my life whom I would not deem worthy.

BE ENCOURAGED

Confirm to your servant your promise,
that you may be feared.
PSALM 119:38 ESV

Sometimes we need a little reassurance of God's love for us. Life is hard, and it is easy to get discouraged when we are persevering in our challenging circumstances but don't feel the hand of God on our efforts. It's a simple truth, however, that the Lord takes pleasure in confirming his love for us as well as the promises which he has made. He loves encouraging us in our walks.

Our challenge today is to ask God to confirm again the things about which he has spoken—a promise from his Word, his calling on our lives. We may ask him for an encouraging word that will speak grace to our hearts. We can be specific in our requests, and therefore witness him proving himself faithful. Time and time again his saints have asked for a word from God, and time and time again he has spoken. Do it today and be encouraged to continue in your pursuit of God.

God, my heart could use encouragement. I ask that you would speak through your Word or a friend and confirm again your faithfulness that my faith may continue to grow.

HOPE AGAINST HOPE

Even when there was no reason for hope, Abraham kept hoping—believing that he would become the father of many nations. For God had said to him, "That's how many descendants you will have!"

ROMANS 4:18 NLT

God has given us countless promises in his Word. The things about which he spoke to his people for generations still hold true for us today. They are the foundation of our hope which is based not in anything this world can offer, but in the eternal nature of a faithful and good God. Our tendency is to forget all the reasons to hope when our earthly pleasures have disappointed us. But God mercifully reminds us that all is not lost according to his promises.

Pray this prayer adapted from Romans 4, placing your own name into the verses that speak of Abraham. May you remember that even when things look bleak in your life, God is still at work, and he is able to accomplish what he has promised you. Hope against hope.

Against hope, with hope I believe. I do not waver in unbelief at God's promise but am strengthened in my faith and give glory to God, because I am fully convinced that what you have promised, you are able to perform.

RIGHTEOUS ANGER

Hot indignation seizes me because of the wicked,
who forsake your law.
PSALM 119:53 ESV

Throughout the Psalms we find descriptions of raw, fully felt and fully embraced emotions. This includes passages where anger is described. One might expect that anger to be felt toward enemies or people who have personally injured the author, but his anger is directed toward those who are not following God and are walking in wicked ways. We can assume that this was not leading him to lash out against them, but to feel a righteous anger that evil persists in this world which leads people away from the truth and the potential for holy living.

How do we respond to those who are not walking in righteousness? If we are honest, can we say that we feel righteous anger when we see God's instructions ignored? Or in our own sin, do we sometimes envy the wicked, trying to make our lives look like theirs while claiming to love God? Does our love for Scripture cause us to abandon all that forsakes God?

God, I am guilty of claiming to love your Word while envying the lives of those who do not follow you. Forgive my hypocrisy and help me walk in purity of heart and mind.

GOODNESS IN LOSS

The LORD is righteous in all his ways,
and kind in all his works.
PSALM 145:17 NASB

Liliana had recently broken up with her boyfriend. She was confused, having been certain that she would marry this man. She was feeling hurt, unloved, and rejected. Together they had sought the Lord and had been moving forward. Now it was suddenly over. As with all hurts, it takes time to heal. One thing Liliana found helped more than anything was thanking the Lord for removing from her life this thing which she had been so convinced was meant to be. She came to see that the Lord is good and righteous in all his ways, and that if something were stripped from her life when she least expected it, she could be thankful that God in his kindness had seen fit to take it away.

How do we respond when something is taken away—a relationship, an opportunity, a hope? While mourning loss has its time (Ecclesiastes 3:4), there also comes time to thank the Lord for choosing better things than we would have chosen for ourselves.

Lord, thank you for being kind enough to take things away from me. While I do not always understand the why, help me to understand your goodness, and accept it with rejoicing.

STRANGERS ON EARTH

I am only a foreigner in the land.
Don't hide your commands from me!
PSALM 119:19 NLT

If you've ever lived in another country or in a culture different from your own, you understand how important it is to educate yourself in the proper way of living with people so different from yourself. Cultural blunders are real, and they can be embarrassing or even appalling. Studying the culture and the people you are living amongst helps you know how to interact in culturally acceptable ways.

As followers of Christ, we are not citizens of this world, but of the kingdom of heaven. As such, the world is not our home, and we need to be informed on the proper way of living here amongst people who are different from us. Just as a cultural guide helps people living in another country, God's Word helps us understand how to live in a world that is not our true home. We can take time today to ground ourselves in the instructions the Scriptures offer so that we are prepared to face all that we will encounter in this world as a foreigner!

God, help me remember that this world is not my final home. I am not meant to fit into this world, but to live according to your Word. Let me hold fast to your instructions.

Called by God

Be sure to fear the LORD
and serve him faithfully with all your heart;
consider what great things he has done for you.
1 SAMUEL 12:24 NIV

It's all too easy to justify a bad day. If we wake up to a cloudy sky when we wanted sun, the day is off to a bad start. When hormones are kicking in hard, we give in to crabbiness. If the unexpected pops up we claim that adulting is too challenging, and we allow ourselves to binge watch our favorite Netflix show to heal the hurt.

But what if, instead of giving in to each bad day, we believe that we have been called by God himself? What if we allow that energy to spur us on toward accountable, dependable, day-to-day living? God's goodness to us is not dependent on us doing things right, and neither does our faithfulness to him need to be dependent on having a good day. We can be faithful whether or not things go according to our plan. We can be determined today to remember who called us, and to live in conviction of that calling!

God, help me, by the power of the Spirit, to walk with consistency today. May my loyalty to you not be determined by my comfort, but by the conviction that you, the God of the universe, have called me!

FIXED ON TRUTH

Even though rulers sit and speak against me,
your servant meditates on your statutes.
PSALM 119:23 NASB

Have you endured speculations and accusations? Have you been mocked because of your lifestyle, your choices, or your faith? It can be so hard to listen to people speak wrongly about you.

In those moments, whose approval do you seek? Do you defend yourself and justify your decisions, hoping to clear your name so you are seen in a positive light? Do you believe what they say, taking on their definitions of who you are? Or do you, like the psalmist, turn to the truth in the Scriptures and fill your mind with what is good and right? When you are wrongly accused, mocked, or bullied, it is vital to go directly to the Word so you can correct your thoughts with the truth of what God says about you. Do not let yourself be undermined by lies; ground yourself in what you know to be true.

Lord, thank you for your Word which reminds me of who I am when others try to define me wrongly. Help me to quickly fill my mind with truth, and not dwell on anything that goes against what you say about me.

LACKING NOTHING

You open your hand;
you satisfy the desire of every living thing.
PSALM 145:16 ESV

Sophia was starting to realize that she tended to fill her time and thoughts with just stuff. It was essentially a demonstration of her lack of faith in God to satisfy her desires. She bought new clothes, spent all her time with friends every weekend, and opened her social media apps anytime she had a spare moment. It all pointed to a disbelief in God's ability to be all she needed. She didn't trust that Jesus was more than enough—that she lacked nothing in him.

What does the way we spend our time and resources say about us? Does it demonstrate satisfaction in God and his care of us, or does it show that we don't trust him to be all we need? Today, let's watch how we spend time and what we fill our minds with. If we give ourselves time to thank God for his provision and care, does it change our mindsets? Spending time today acknowledging his goodness and faithfulness will remind us that he is our Shepherd, and all we need (Psalm 23:1).

Lord, forgive me for filling my thoughts and time with things instead of allowing myself to dwell on the sufficiency of Christ. Help me believe that you are the best thing.

EMBRACING THE UNKNOWN

When I am afraid,
I will trust you.
PSALM 56:3 NCV

Sometimes it seems that God doesn't want us playing it safe in life. Many of us love our comfort, and we do our best to keep ourselves in calm waters close to the proverbial shoreline. We avoid things that cause pain. We stick to a well laid plan. But God isn't as interested in our safety and comfort as we are. He calls us into unknown situations, where the future is unclear, and we have to rely on him to be the lamp to our path. He changes our plans and leads us into circumstances that are sometimes painful but cause us to depend on him fully.

Be certain of this, friend. That scary, unknown situation which God has led you into is so much safer than the calm, clearly marked road of your own choosing. Embrace the hard things that he has planned, knowing that they will bring goodness and reward if you follow him. He is worth trusting!

Lord, help me trust you when I am afraid. These challenging situations that I would not have chosen for myself will bring goodness to my life and glory to you, so help me rely on your Spirit and to fully embrace each moment.

Praiseworthy

Fix your thoughts on what is true, and honorable, and right, and pure, and lovely, and admirable. Think about things that are excellent and worthy of praise.

PHILIPPIANS 4:8 NLT

The news is a daily reminder of all that is wrong with the world. It's true that we are living in times when lawlessness abounds, when God's instructions are ignored or mocked, and when the believer is made to feel like the enemy. But we need to remember that no matter what the current situation is in the world, we are always living in the midst of God's grace. Nothing in the world can change the fact that we have an inheritance in the age to come.

Therefore, let's set our minds on what is good, true, and worthy of giving God praise for his grace which sustains us. We are so grateful for his love which never grows tired, and the promise of eternity in glory with the saints. We do not need to get bogged down with all that is wrong in the world. We can turn our eyes upon Jesus daily and remember to acknowledge all that is praiseworthy in him.

Lord, what a comfort to know that regardless of the present circumstances, I know that my future is secure. Help me keep my focus on you and the promise of glory, filling my mind with all that is true and worthy of praise.

MARCH

He made him ride
on the heights of the land
and fed him with
the fruit of the fields.
He nourished him with
honey from the rock.

DEUTERONOMY 32:13 NIV

COUNSEL

I will praise the LORD, who counsels me;
even at night my heart instructs me.
PSALM 16:7 NIV

We all know that our hearts are not the most reliable teachers. We are swayed by emotions and wrongful desires, and we're told by the world to follow our hearts; this often leads us into sin. But God is the Creator of the heart, and he has good purposes for it too. In Psalms, David often speaks of his heart counseling or instructing him. Why would David allow his heart to instruct him? The Lord speaks through our hearts by nudging our consciences and calling us back to righteousness when we are moving toward sin.

Through the Word and through our consciences, God instructs us in the right way to live. For that we praise him! Praise God that he does not abandon us to figure out life on our own or leave us walking in sin without reminding us of what is right and good. Praise God that he has given us his Word which is living and active and speaks to our spirits.

God, how good you are to give us your Word and to speak to our hearts when we need to hear from you. Let me never take that for granted. May I, like David, bless the Lord who counsels me!

THE GIFT OF AFFLICTION

It is good for me that I have been afflicted,
that I may learn your statutes.
PSALM 119:71 NKJV

Some of us woke this morning to a relatively normal day.
We have our challenges as all days do, but life is somewhat
stable. Others woke this morning to their world falling apart.
Loss has met them. Heartbreak has shattered their souls. For
them, the battle is exponentially more difficult than they
would have chosen for themselves. Each of us can think
upon our trials in two ways: we can see them as afflictions
that cause our hearts to grow in bitterness, or we can see
them as gifts that cause our souls to grow in maturity.

When have you been able to see that affliction has
proven to be a good thing? What have you learned about
God through challenges that you might have otherwise
missed? Today, whether your battle is great or small, thank
the Lord for it, mourn if you need to, and determine that
you will not miss what God has appointed for you to learn.

Lord, you know so much better than I how to shape my
heart. Help me see my trials today in the light of your grace,
that I might not miss out on becoming more like Jesus.

ROAD CLOSED

I wait for the Lord, my soul waits,
and in his word I hope.
PSALM 130:5 ESV

Imagine you are on a road trip with your family. You have
an exciting destination awaiting you and you can't wait
to get there. The trip should only be about twelve hours,
but within an hour of starting it is clear that this won't be a
straightforward journey. Detours, traffic stops, and engine
trouble cause delay after delay.

That's how life feels sometimes, right? What should be
straightforward and easy turns out to be one delay or
detour after another. When frustration starts to arise in
our hearts, our capacity for patience depends on our
ability to believe in God's purposes. He is at work creating
something good for us in all of the interruptions by taking
us by the "long way." Today, we can thank him for the
delays in our days. We can thank him for changing our
routes. We don't yet know what mercy is being shown to
us on our journey.

Lord, help me by the power of your Spirit to be patient
and believe that you are in control even when things
aren't going as it seems they should. I know you are good.

ADVOCATE

For you bless the righteous person, Lord,
you surround him with favor as with a shield.

PSALM 5:12 NASB

Consider the word *advocate* for a moment. An advocate according to the dictionary, is "one who pleads another's cause," or as a verb it is, "to plead in favor of." Jesus pleads in favor of us before the Father; he went to the full extent in advocating for us in order to remove God's divine wrath from his people and to have it directed toward himself instead. What amazing grace!

Think about how you can be an advocate for those in your own life. Are you looking for opportunities to defend your brothers and sisters? Do you seek to surround them with favor, to plead their cause, to bless them? People are too often caught up in their own opinions and their own causes to defend those of someone else. Ask the Lord how you can honor and be an advocate for someone in need today.

Lord, you defended me when I was in sin, going so far as to take the punishment that I deserved upon yourself. Help me, Spirit, to treat others that same way, blessing and honoring others instead of defending myself.

Ever-Present Help

God is our refuge and strength,
an ever-present help in trouble.
Therefore we will not fear, though the earth give way
and the mountains fall into the heart of the sea.
PSALM 46:1-2 NIV

God is an ever-present help in trouble. How comforting is that? We do not serve a God who stands aside and watches our pain; he interacts, he comes to our aid, he comforts and provides strength. We can pray this verse for ourselves today, entering in the things in our own lives with which God is helping us through:

Therefore, we will not fear…

- though our relationships with our families are struggling, or
- though we wait in uncertainty about the future, or
- though we don't know how to share our faith with others, or
- though the pain of loss colors our days.

In all circumstances, God's presence is our good. May this truth bring confidence in Christ and freedom to trust him implicitly.

Jesus, I am so thankful for your presence with me in my circumstances. Help me not to fear, for you are with me.

NO GOOD APART FROM GOD

"You are my LORD;
I have no good apart from you."
PSALM 16:2 ESV

A prayer for you today:

The faithfulness of the Lord is all around you. Throughout your day may God show you all the small things he does, that you may be reminded of his steadfast and everlasting passion for your heart. May your intimacy with God grow powerfully as you walk by faith into his will for you. By that great love, may you walk without fear or hesitation but with great delight into the arms of a capable God.

May your obedience overcome the frailties of humanity. May you seek pleasure from no other sources. May you be okay with Christ—the supreme pleasure and joy. May you rest securely in the knowledge that you are thoroughly and sincerely loved by God. May he be your goodness and light—and that apart from him you have nothing at all.

Oh Lord, help me to know in my innermost being that you are my source of good and all joy. Let me walk confidently because I am rescued by grace and kept by love.

PERSPECTIVE ON THE WORD

I have rejoiced in your laws
as much as in riches.
PSALM 119:14 NLT

The psalmist repeatedly speaks of God's Word as that
which he delights in, trusts, treasures, and rejoices over. He
studies it because he sees it as life-giving. He finds comfort
in it. He hurries to obey it. What dedication to God's Word!
How does this compare to your own view of the Word? Do
you see God's decrees as rich and something to be sought
after? Is it something you long to study and meditate on
because you understand the good that comes from that?
Or does the Word feel more like a series of killjoy rules that
prevent you from living as you would choose?

Our opinion of God's Word colors the entire way we live,
and the wrong perspective will cause us to miss out on the
blessings of obedience and of really knowing God. We need
to ask ourselves today how we see the Word. Is it truth,
which we have fully dedicated ourselves to pursuing?

Lord, help me see your Word as it truly is: a treasure worth
pursuing with all my heart. May I seek you and find all your
promises to be true.

STEADFAST LOVE

The steadfast love of the LORD never ceases;
his mercies never come to an end;
they are new every morning;
great is your faithfulness.
LAMENTATIONS 3:22-23 ESV

If you have had any amount of human interaction in your life, you understand the irregularity with which people love one another. You can be best friends at one moment, and worst enemies the next. You adore your children, but they are driving you crazy and you only want to be alone. Your coworker treats you with kindness one day, and the next you can't do anything right. Humanity is fickle, and our love is therefore capricious.

Imagine if God loved us the same way. If his love were based on our ability to love with consistency, we'd be sunk. Instead, his love is steadfast, unwavering, and not at all dependent on our propensity to do things right. We can thank him for that love today and ask him to empower us to demonstrate that same love to those in our lives.

God, I am anything but reliable, but I am so thankful that your faithfulness is not dependent on me. Thank you for your persistent love which never changes despite my inconsistencies. Teach me to love like you do.

ABOUNDING GRACE

God is able to make all grace overflow to you, so that,
always having all sufficiency in everything, you may have
an abundance for every good deed.

2 CORINTHIANS 9:8 NASB

You are abounding in grace, friend. Never does God leave
you in want. You have all that you need available to you
for all your needs at all times. What a gift! What needs do
you have today? Ask the Lord for his overflowing grace
to prove all-sufficient in your life. Are you feeling heavy,
overwhelmed, or anxious? Ask the Lord to sustain you for
every good work which he has planned for you today.

The incredible thing about our God is that he does not
stand around watching us struggle; he is near to the
brokenhearted, he makes grace abound when we need it,
he strengthens us, he gives all we need. Accept that truth
for yourself today and take your stand in it.

God, thank you for not being stingy with your grace.
Thank you that I do not have to earn it. Thank you that you
provide for my every need each and every day. Help me
stand fast in your grace.

PRAISE ALL THE TIME

Because the LORD is great; he should be praised at all times.
He should be honored more than all the gods.

PSALM 96:4 NCV

Millie woke with a song of praise in her heart. She knew it was a gracious reminder of the need to look to the Lord today, to give him glory in the ordinary things of her day. What she didn't know was that her day would take an unexpected turn. For a time, in the midst of confusion, the sudden pain, and the shock of the unforeseen, she forgot about the worshipful attitude she had when she awoke that morning. But the Lord mercifully brought to her mind again the praise that had been on her lips when everything had been calm and peaceful.

The Lord is great; therefore, he is worthy of our praise at all times. How often do we praise the Lord when all is well, but promptly forget to worship when things take a turn for the worse? Can we, like Job, say with integrity and joy, "The Lord gave these things to me, and he has taken them away. Praise the name of the Lord" (Job 1:21)?

Lord, you are worthy of praise all the time and in all circumstances. Forgive me for only praising you when things are going well, but abandoning my worship when challenges arise. Give me a spirit of worship regardless of what comes my way today.

CONSTANT

Do not cast me off in the time of old age;
forsake me not when my strength is spent.
PSALM 71:9 ESV

Perhaps you are young and capable; old age seems a lifetime away. Or perhaps you are now nearing your later years and feeling your body change. Regardless of your current age, there will come a time in life when you find yourself less capable than you once were—the strength of youth fades, perhaps taken prematurely by disease or injury. Our earthly bodies are perpetual reminders of the frailty of the human condition and of our dependence on a God who is not held back by human constraints.

There is beauty in knowing that our God's character is constant and will never change even as we do. He does not get weaker as time goes on. He is no less capable a hundred years from now as he is today. His faithfulness to guide, protect, and care for his children will never fail because he is unchanging. Praise him today for his constancy.

God, what comfort in knowing that even as my body and mind weaken, your strength remains the same. Thank you for loving me, not because I am capable, but because you are good.

THE NATURE OF THE WORD

Forever, O LORD,
your word is settled in heaven.
PSALM 119:89 NKJV

Here is one of the miracles of the Word of God: nothing can spoil it, change it, or cause any of it to become untrue. Psalm 119 says that it is settled—firmly fixed—in heaven. Outside of time, the elements of decay and away from the powers of darkness, the Words of the Lord are safe and unchanging. And yet, they are available to us! What else in life is like that?

It is easy to take Scripture for granted because it is so readily available to us. But it is something to be treasured and treated with respect. In it are the Words of the everlasting God. Are we all prepared to give it the honor which it deserves?

God, the nature of your Word is so unlike anything else in my life. Thank you for preserving it through the centuries so that your truth may speak to all generations. Help me by the power of your Spirit to honor it, pursue it, and obey it through all of life's ups and downs.

GOING AFTER GOOD

My heart says of you, "Seek his face!"
Your face, LORD, I will seek.
PSALM 27:8 NIV

We all get stuck in a funk from time to time. Challenges, moods, and cloudy days combine to pull our souls out of the joy of the Lord and into introspective spirals. We begin to see only what is wrong with our current lives. In those times, it is vital that we do what is good for us: we need to seek the Lord. When we seek his face, the heaviness of our current issues fades and dim. We will accurately see the great things as great, and the small things as small.

We rejoice in today! We do not wish that the Lord had called us to something he didn't; we embrace our calling—the joy and the pain of it—and we do not live in a way so as to regret any moment given to us. Pursuing Christ is the most important thing we can ever do.

Jesus, you faced every temptation that I now face, so you understand feelings of lethargy and wishing for things that are not mine to have. In those moments, please help me to take hold of the joy that you offer when I seek your face.

GIFT OF UNDERSTANDING

You made me and formed me with your hands.
Give me understanding so I can learn your commands.
PSALM 119:73 NCV

What things are you passionate about? What drives your desire to learn, to grow in understanding? What gets you excited to discover more and go deeper? The ability to learn and pursue knowledge are gifts from God; his creation is discoverable, and we were made to discover it! But what does the Bible tell us about learning? The psalmist asks for understanding not so he could pursue the things that sparked his interest, but so that he could learn the commands of God.

While our passions are certainly gifts, it is always important to come back to the foundational reason the Lord gave us the ability to learn. He is a God that we can know. He is discoverable. His Word holds promises, revelations, ideas that no man could come up with. Scripture is full of good commands that we can give ourselves to in discovery. We need to make sure that our passions do not cloud out the joy of pursuing understanding of the Word.

God, thank you for giving me a mind to explore, discover, and learn about your creation. Thank you for the gift of passion and finding enjoyment in learning.

THE PERFECT PLACE

The LORD longs to be gracious to you,
and therefore he waits on high
to have compassion on you.
For the LORD is a God of justice;
how blessed are all those who long for him.
ISAIAH 30:18 NASB

Do you ever wish your life were different? In this age of social media and "Insta-perfect" lives, it is too easy to compare your life to someone else's. It's tempting to see the good and the beautiful in their existence but fail to see the pain they suffer or the battles they fight. The phone and the computer is a highlight reel of the green grass in strangers' lives, and it leaves the reader discontent and feeling like God has blessed someone else more than you.

When Satan tempts you to this viewpoint, remember this: God has you where you are because it is good. He longs to be gracious to you. God brought you to this place at this time because he is sovereign, good, and merciful, and he has your best interests in mind. That doesn't mean that giddiness and happiness infuse every moment of every day, but it does mean you can trust him that this day and all that is in it is the best thing for you.

God, help me to accept this place and time in my life as the perfect thing which you know I need. You are trustworthy and good.

AFFLICTED BY FAITHFULNESS

I know, O Lord, that your rules are righteous,
and that in faithfulness you have afflicted me.
PSALM 119:75 ESV

Life can be so disappointing. You plan and anticipate good things that fall through at the worst possible times. It can all feel so unfair. When disappointments happen in life, do you trust in God's good and righteous judgement, or do you accuse him of being unfair? How do the people in your life see you respond to disappointments? Are you tossed about on the waves of emotion when hopes and expectations come to nothing? Or do people see that you are not easily moved because you so strongly trust in the goodness of God?

The psalmist wrote that he knows it is due to the faithfulness of God that affliction comes into his life. That's a strong statement. He knew that God can be blamed for nothing, but that his judgements are fair and trustworthy. The next time disappointment comes your way, meet it with a declaration of your trust in your good and faithful God.

Lord, your faithfulness keeps me afloat when the storms of life are rocking me. Thank you for allowing affliction, trouble, and disappointment so that I remember to set my hope on you alone.

YET TO COME

"The LORD is my portion," says my soul,
"Therefore I wait for him."
LAMENTATIONS 3:24 NASB

You are not like those "whose portion is in this life" (Psalm 17:14). Think about that. For some people—many people actually—the joys of the present world are the best they will ever get. For you who belong to the Lord, the treasures of this world do not compare to the riches of knowing Christ and dwelling in his kingdom forever. And yet how often do you trade the glory of knowing God for the best that this fallen world can offer?

Would you not be insulted if a friend continually chose to spend time with someone else rather than with you? That is what people do all the time to God, showing that they prefer everything else to him. Yet he is not proud. He does not shut down when they have once again tried to make their portion in this world only. Instead, he graciously opens his arms and waits for them to return. What love!

God, how gracious you are to me, taking me back when I repeatedly set my sights on the things of this world. Forgive me for living as if life here is the best it will get for me. Help me take every opportunity to pursue you. I will not be disappointed!

PROMISE OF COMFORT

Let your steadfast love comfort me
according to your promise to your servant.
PSALM 119:76 ESV

The pain was immense and unexpected. Molly didn't think that she would feel so strongly for someone else's suffering, but here it was—utter heartbreak. Years of prayers and hopes culminated in a day of sudden loss and extreme sorrow. Where was God on days like this?

While it can be tempting to think that in our heartbreak God has distanced himself, the opposite is actually true. He promises that he will not forsake us, not on the days when we are doing well, and not on the days when our hearts break. He is called the God of all comfort (2 Corinthians 1:3), and he keeps track of our sorrows and catches our tears in his bottle (Psalm 56:8). His steadfast love brings comfort to the weary and heals the bruised hearts of his people. If we are in pain today, we can ask for his comfort. We can pray for his nearness. It is a promise which we will receive.

Lord, thank you for understanding my sorrow, and promising comfort. Help me take hold of the hope your presence brings, and rest in the comfort you offer my aching heart.

Fear of God or Man

The eyes of the LORD are on those who fear him,
on those whose hope is in his unfailing love.
PSALM 33:18 NIV

Society tells us that other people's opinions of us are
important even though we are also told not to care about
what other people think of us. Fear of man will always be
an issue until the fear of God takes root in our hearts. We
need to check our motives for the way we spend our time
so we can determine who we actually fear. Do we spend
a lot of time taking care of our bodies because we care
about what people think about our looks? Do we spend
time with certain people because we care about who we
are seen with? Do we spend more time wondering what
people think about us than we do thinking about the
Lord's opinion of us?

When our hearts are right before the Lord and we are
pursuing him, nothing else matters. We are then able to
focus our energy on loving him and walking in a way that
is worthy of his calling. We want to please him and not
worry about pleasing anyone else. Their thoughts of us are
not eternal, but those of God are!

Lord, I want to be a woman who fears the Lord and not
man. Help me keep my eyes on you, to care about the
condition of my heart toward you, and to place my hope
in your faithful love.

READING FOR PURPOSE

Teach me, Lord, the way of your decrees,
that I may follow it to the end.
PSALM 119:33 NIV

It happens to us all: half-awake, we grab our coffee and
Bibles. We want to start the day with Jesus because we
know it is good. We read through the passage twice or
three times, but the words are only partially absorbed
into our tired minds, and we keep moving on, praying a
quick prayer for the day ahead. As the day goes on, we
have absolutely no idea what we read that morning. Good
intentions led us to start our day with Jesus, but if we are
spending that time in the Word to check off a spiritual to-
do list, we need a new approach.

The psalmist prayed that the Lord would teach him his
decrees so that he may follow them. Friend, are you
reading with the intention to obey? Is your time with
Jesus reflective of a mind that truly wants to understand
and follow what is read, or are you caught in the doing-it-
to-do-it mindset? Ask the Holy Spirit to help you read his
inspired Word with the intention and focus that it deserves!

God, I am guilty of spending time in the Word just to say
I did. Forgive me and help me find a new way to spend
time with you which will benefit my relationship with you
long-term.

HOLDING ON TO HOPE

All these people are known for their faith, but none of them received what God had promised. God planned to give us something better so that they would be made perfect, but only together with us.

HEBREWS 11:39-40 NCV

Do you ever find yourself dreaming of the "good old days?" The past appeals to us because the memories bring feelings of familiarity and comfort. We tend to remember the good, and in our mind's eye we see the past in a rosy-colored light that is not tainted with memories of the difficulties that also were a part of our days. This longing is in our hearts because God created us for eternity with him, not just this present age.

But if you find yourself dreaming of the "good old days" or just challenged by your current discomfort, remember that hundreds of generations of other Christ-followers have also yearned for eternity with the Father. What was their secret in pressing on despite imperfect situations? They maintained their faith in a good God whom they knew would be faithful to fulfill his promises even if they never actually saw them fulfilled in this lifetime.

God, thank you for the stories of so many who lived through the challenges of life and did so with complete faith in your promises. Help me also to keep my eyes focused on the author and perfecter of my faith.

DETERMINED TO OVERCOME

Faith by itself, if it does not have works, is dead.
JAMES 2:17 NKJV

When gloomy days come into our minds, this is the combination that we should reach for: a good dose of determination, and a whole lot of the Holy Spirit. We will never kick moodiness to the curb for good. We are human and will continue to struggle until our sinful nature is completely done away with.

But we also do not need to be controlled by moods or the complaining spirit that tends to overtake us when things have gone awry. Praying alone doesn't usually send those attitudes away but asking the Holy Spirit for the power to do what is right coupled with a determination to start moving in the right direction is often enough of the kick-start we need to get back on track. Today, we just need to ask the Spirit for the power to choose a joyful attitude, and then *get moving*.

God, it is easier to sit in my moodiness than it is to overcome it, but I know that you came so I might have an abundant life. Help me, therefore, to reach for your power and to do my part in pursuing a holy life.

KNOWING GOD

How abundant is your goodness,
which you have stored up for those who fear you
and worked for those who take refuge in you,
in the sight of the children of mankind!

PSALM 31:19 ESV

When getting to know someone, it is often the good
qualities that initially stand out and draw us to them.
When we read the Scripture and learn about the character
of God, it is the good and beautiful traits that draw us into
knowing him and loving him. This allows us to see God
as close to us and a real source of our joy in life. He's not
just some far off idea. Knowing him spurs our hearts on to
pursuing him. Psalm 31 lists some of the characteristics of
God that we find amazing:

- he is abundantly good,
- he protects,
- he leads and guides,
- his love is faithful, and
- he knows my troubles but does not hand me over to
  the enemy.

Take time to get to know your God according to the Word.

Lord, how good you are to give me insight into who you
are. Open my heart to understanding your Word, so that I
might know you better.

BLAMELESS

May my heart be blameless in your statutes,
so that I will not be ashamed.
PSALM 119:80 NASB

Why is it always easier to see everyone else's issues? We tend to be blind to our own struggles, weaknesses, and faults, but we see clearly the flaws of those around us! God knew our tendency to find fault with the world while missing our own but praise him that his mercy is new for us each day.

Today, consider how you might be pointing the finger of blame at someone, or highlighting the weakness of those around you, all while failing to see your own struggles. Ask the Holy Spirit to reveal the darkness of your own heart, so that you can repent and walk in blamelessness. Remember that the actions of those around you are never an excuse for you to walk in unrighteousness. Make sure you are right before the Lord, and his goodness and justice will take care of everyone else.

Lord, forgive me for paying more attention to the faults of those around me rather than addressing my own weaknesses. Help me see my sin as sin so that I can repent and walk in your ways.

CHEERING YOU ON

If we confess our sins, he is faithful and just and will
forgive us our sins and purify us from all unrighteousness.
1 JOHN 1:9 NIV

Our struggle with the sinful nature can wear us down. It is
hard to fight day after day and still find ourselves besieged
with the same thoughts, actions, or behaviors that show
our rebellious hearts toward God. It seems that our own
patience in dealing with sin is far shorter than that of the
Lord, but it is his kindness that leads us back to repentance.
It encourages us to keep fighting the good fight.

Think about this: Jesus is not sitting in heaven, tapping
his foot, and thinking, "Come on now, pull it together!"
Instead, he sees your weak steps and glances toward
him and says, "Yes, yes, yes! Keep going, my love!" He is
cheering you on. There is not an ounce of disappointment
in his heart when you stumble once again. He has only joy
and pride. Let that encourage you to keep returning to
him and to keep confessing to him. He is faithful and just
and he will forgive and purify you!

God, I am so humbled by your love for a sinner like me.
Thank you for never seeing me with impatience. Help me
walk in confidence of your great pleasure in me.

RESPOND

The Lord is great and worthy of our praise;
no one can understand how great he is.

PSALM 145:3 NCV

The goal of the Christian life comes down to one task: respond properly to the character of God in all circumstances. Did you recently lose your job? Your job is to praise God for his provision. Has sickness or weakness ravaged your body? Your job is to thank him for his sovereignty. Are you struggling in a relationship? Your job is to acknowledge God's goodness.

Regardless of your circumstances, God's character remains the same. No matter what you are facing in life, he is worthy of your worship. Respond to his character each day and in every situation. Acknowledge his goodness, grace, faithfulness, kindness, sovereignty, and power. He is the God who is able to do exceedingly more than you can anticipate and go beyond all you could ask or dream. He goes above and beyond that which is above and beyond that which is above and beyond! That is the God you serve, and he is worthy of your praise.

Lord, regardless of what I face today or whatever comes my way, help me respond rightly to you. You are worthy of all the glory and honor no matter what the circumstances of my day are, and you are fully in control.

TRUST HIS HAND

Those who know your name put their trust in you,
for you, O LORD, have not forsaken those who seek you.

PSALM 9:10 ESV

It is by the grace of God that we experience joyful,
pleasant seasons in life. We enjoy the sweet summer days
of the Christian walk when we feel the presence of the
Lord, taste the sweetness of good things, and find beauty
in his world. Those days are gifts, but as with all things,
they do not last forever.

Perhaps change has come your way which may not have
been anticipated or welcome. But be encouraged, friend,
to walk with confidence into whatever new season awaits
you. Do not regret that life moves on; there are only ever
good things in store for the ones who love God. That does
not mean that your days will be easy or always enjoyable,
but you can trust the hand of the one who leads you
onward—it is *good*.

God, it is hard to let go of the seasons of life which have
been filled with joy and good things but help me to trust
that you are in control of my days, and you will not forsake
me as I move forward.

POWER OF WEAKNESS

"My grace is all you need. My power works best in weakness." So now I am glad to boast about my weaknesses, so that the power of Christ can work through me.

2 CORINTHIANS 12:9 NLT

Much of the Christian life entails choosing an attitude of hope and joy despite the circumstances around us. Satan waits for every opportunity to trip us up, discourage us, and dish out fear and defeat. When a spirit of heaviness comes over us and Satan's lies become easy to believe, we can find victory by speaking the truth about ourselves as God's daughters and our places in the world.

Life is challenging, yes. We are being broken, humbled, and made beautiful like God. We need not complain about that—it is something to rejoice in! His grace is sufficient for us; let's have confidence in God's goodness to empower us to face whatever comes our way today. We will speak his truth, take hold of his power, and watch him overcome!

God, forgive me for allowing my hope to waver in the face of difficulty. Give me strength to choose to hope, rejoice, and thank in the midst of life's demands. May your power rest on me in my weakness today.

WORSHIP

Praise the LORD, all nations on earth.
Praise the LORD's glory and power.
1 CHRONICLES 16:28 NCV

Our lives are made for worship, and it doesn't happen only in church on Sunday mornings. Every day we give ourselves in worship to something—ourselves, other people, creation, or God. If the only "worship" we recognize happens with other believers, there's a pretty good chance that we are allowing other things to fill the place of worship in our hearts the rest of the time.

When we are giving our time to our own agendas and to things that promote ourselves, our worship is of us. When we are allowing the ideas and desires of other people to govern our decisions, worship is of them. And if our minds are always filled with the things we hope to accomplish and going after the things of the world, we are worshipping creation rather than the Creator. We can be sure, however, that our minds are filled with things that will worship the Lord by taking certain steps. Meditate on the Word. Give thanks to God. Go for a walk and take notice of the glorious things God has made. Setting our hearts on worshipping the Lord every day.

God, you are worthy of all glory and honor. Help me give myself to the worship of you alone.

Not About Us

These are written so that you may believe that Jesus is the Christ, the Son of God, and that by believing you may have life in his name.

JOHN 20:31 ESV

We all love talking about ourselves. Even the introverts amongst us have to admit that it's pleasurable to share stories about life and experiences. The unfortunate consequence of this tendency is that we bring it into our Bible readings. Most of us tend to make the Bible about us—telling us who we are and what we should do, looking to it for the answers to all our questions about ourselves. While the Bible certainly does those things, it is not the primary purpose of God's Word.

Our time in the Bible should be spent seeking God—getting to know him, understanding his character, and knowing what he has done and will do. It should not primarily be a "how-to" for our own lives or finding out more about ourselves. We should be considerate about how we read the Bible. We should make sure we are spending time in God's Word seeking answers more about him than about ourselves, and there we will find true blessing.

Lord, I am sorry for making your Word about me. Your Word is a gift that I might know you and have life in your name. Holy Spirit, help me read the Bible with the purpose of knowing you more.

DELIGHT

He rescued me, because he delighted in me.
PSALM 18:19 NASB

Sarah was in a difficult life season for an extended period of time. She waited, prayed, and hoped for the fulfillment of a good, God-given dream, and yet her hopes were continually dashed. She still trusted in God's goodness, but she needed a reminder that she meant more to God than her unfulfilled dream.

In Psalm 18 she read this verse: "He rescued me, because he delighted in me." This was the breath of fresh air that Sarah needed as she sat with open hands, holding her dreams loosely while holding tightly to the hand of her God. God delighted in her. He was pleased with her, not because of anything that she had done and not because she persevered in her hopes, but because she was his. Do you know his delight in you today? His rescue might not always mean relief, or the dream achieved at long last. But his pleasure in you will draw him near and bring fullness of joy (Psalm 16:11).

Lord, thank you for seeing me with eyes of delight. You love me. I am yours. There is nothing that can cause you to look at me with anything but adoration. Draw near to me today that I may experience absolute fullness of joy in your presence.

APRIL

He would feed you
with the finest of wheat,
and with honey from the rock
I would satisfy you.

PSALM 81:16 ESV

COMPASSION IN WEAKNESS

Have compassion on me, Lord, for I am weak.
PSALM 6:2 NLT

This verse can be our plea in so many situations. In the weaknesses of our bodies causing hardship throughout the day, or in the weaknesses of our minds during a wearisome emotional season, we cry out to God for compassion. Or perhaps it is a cry for help with a situation that is out of our control, and we know all too well how incapable we are of doing anything on our own.

We are often faced with our weaknesses when we least expect it or when it is the least convenient. Maybe the Lord does that purposely; he knows our desire for independence and individuality. But the reminders of our weaknesses are not just so God can show his strength but so he can show his compassion. He loves to hide us in the shadow of his wings. He delights in rescuing us. He is our rock and our refuge, and he wants to be that safe place for us. If weaknesses overwhelm us today, we can call out for God's compassionate strength.

Thank you, Lord, that you are a compassionate and gracious God. Thank you for being slow to anger and abounding in love and faithfulness. May your compassion cover me in the moments of my weaknesses so that you may receive glory.

LONGING

Faith is confidence in what we hope for and assurance
about what we do not see.

HEBREWS 11:1 NIV

Perhaps you find in yourself a steady discontent with life.
When you're home, you long for adventure; when you
finally have the chance to go see the world, you desire
the comfort of home. When you have mountains, you
want the sea. When you're young and single, you wish
for a family of your own; as a married person, you want
independence. If this is you, you must take these longings
as a clear indication of the reason your hope *must not* be
built on earthly things. They will disappoint tremendously.

Your affections must be set on Christ alone who will not
disappoint, and you will find that your hope does not
waver. All that you need is invisible to the eye. So don't
look for it, not here.

Lord, my longings tell me that I have yet to set my hope
and affections fully on you. I will continually be let down
until I have fixed my eyes on that which I cannot see—the
hope of eternity with you. Help me not look for fulfillment
here on earth but to pursue you alone as the one who can
satisfy my desires.

Go For Growth

The way you live will always honor and please the Lord, and your lives will produce every kind of good fruit. All the while, you will grow as you learn to know God better and better.

COLOSSIANS 1:10 NLT

Do you ever find yourself in a stagnant place in your relationship with the Lord? Life has a way of taking over your thoughts and practices, and unless you are actively pursuing Christ, your relationship with him will begin to feel stale.

Remember that the time you take to seek God will be proportionate to the growth in your relationship with him. This idea can take a while to be fully realized; a good relationship always takes time and effort. It requires sacrifices. It takes purposeful study. Relationships flourish when a person becomes a student of the one they love. If your relational roots are shallow, you will not withstand the storms of life. If you find yourself in a rut, it is possible that you are not giving the Lord the time and attention needed in order to grow. Set aside some time every day for the next week to really study and meditate on the character of God; growth is sure to follow.

Jesus, sometimes I allow life to take over, and I neglect the time I need seeking you. Help me remember there is no better use of my time than spending it in your Word and in prayer.

REPENTANCE

In Christ we are set free by the blood of his death, and so
we have forgiveness of sins. How rich is God's grace, which
he has given to us so fully and freely.

EPHESIANS 1:7-8 NCV

The world and the devil specifically will try to tell you
that because of your sin you are a failure; you will never
amount to anything. You might as well give up trying
to walk righteously because God surely doesn't want
you. These lies combined with pride are the perfect
combination for a reluctance to repent of sin. Be assured,
friend. This couldn't be further from the truth.

Scripture says that Christ's blood purchased freedom
for you, and it happened while you were dead in your
trespasses (Ephesians 2:1). Repentance is, in essence,
a way of making your mistakes, a difficult past, or a
complicated present, a starting point for something new
and something better. God's grace has not been removed
from you because of your mistakes. Do not believe the lies
that tell you that you will never overcome. Get up, seek
forgiveness, and go for something better.

Lord, I am so undeserving of your grace, but thank you
for lavishing it on me! How humbling it is that you see my
mistakes as a starting point for something better. Help me
take hold of the opportunity to grow.

FEEL-GOOD BOOK

The law of the LORD is perfect,
refreshing the soul.
The statutes of the LORD are trustworthy,
making wise the simple.
PSALM 19:7 NIV

One result of our egocentric society is the tendency to read the Bible for the comfort of our hearts. Now don't get me wrong; God's Word does comfort our hearts! We are told repeatedly that God is near to those who are hurting, and he comforts us in our trouble. But the Bible doesn't exist *just* to comfort us. If you define success in reading the Bible by finding something that makes you feel good, then you need to revise your Bible-reading objectives.

God's Word exists not only to encourage us in times of difficulty, but to equip us for good works. It communicates essential thinking that prepares us for battle against the enemy. It also corrects us in our errors and convicts us of our sins. Honestly, we should expect to be made *uncomfortable* by what we read because this means that the Spirit of God is at work making us aware of the need for grace. Praise God when his Word causes us to mourn our sin. Praise God when we realize that we are missing the mark. Celebrate the Word which makes us grow!

God, help me to not fall into the pattern of reading your Word for my own comfort. You want so much more for me than to feel good!

Not Disappointed

This hope will not lead to disappointment. For we know how dearly God loves us, because he has given us the Holy Spirit to fill our hearts with his love.

ROMANS 5:5 NLT

Another day, another disappointment. Isn't that how it feels sometimes? The pain of sin, weariness in doing good without a foreseeable harvest, expectations that come to nothing: the list goes on and on of the things that afflict our minds on a daily basis. Will you cave to the pressure of disenchantment? Will you allow yourself to be crushed and give up hope that God is still good?

Friend, you have to decide in your will to remain hopeful. You probably won't come out on top if you just wait for the pain to leave. Choose to rejoice. Act on the hope buried under this present sadness and worship the One who is worthy. Overcome these attitudes by turning your attention toward your only hope, which is in Jesus Christ. Do it now. Salvation and all these blessings of a life in Christ is yours. It is the ultimate source of hope.

God, thank you for allowing trials to enter my life. May I choose to let them do their work of building endurance, strength of character, and most of all, confident hope in your salvation! Strengthen me by your Spirit to choose to rejoice despite the pain!

HIS PERFECT WAY

This God—his way is perfect;
the word of the LORD proves true;
he is a shield for all those who take refuge in him.
PSALM 18:30 ESV

Jamie realized as a teenager that being under her parents' authority also meant being under their protection. If she took matters into her own hands and decided to leave their authority, it meant that things might happen that they could not protect her from. It was a revelation that she carried with her into adulthood, and into her relationship with the Lord.

Psalms tells us that God's way is perfect. *Perfect* means without flaw or fault, as good as it possibly can be. It also tells us that those who put themselves under the command of his perfect way are protected. Following God's perfect way, as shown to us in his Word, means that we are putting ourselves under God's authority and therefore under his protection. Just as Jamie was under the watchful protection of her parents as long as she was keeping herself under their authority, so too are we under the protection of the all-powerful God as we follow his perfect way.

Lord, thank you for the promise of protection when I am walking in righteousness.

UNSHAKEN

I keep my eyes always on the LORD.
With him at my right hand, I will not be shaken.
Therefore my heart is glad and my tongue rejoices;
my body also will rest secure.

PSALM 16:8-9 NIV

Emotions are powerful. They can cause us to make life-altering decisions, react strongly to various events, or carry us through difficulties. They can also cause us to fall into despair. As Jesus-followers, we know that our emotions are not to rule our hearts; that is Christ's job. God is to be the one directing us by the fact of his lordship. We are not to be led by the feelings that rise up when things happen, whether good or bad.

In Psalm 16, David said that he always kept his eyes on the Lord, knowing that with him he was not shaken. When we focus our attention on the Lord and consciously set our minds on him, we practice thankfulness and acknowledge his presence. We are not surprised or caught off guard by the disturbances that regularly upset the flow of life. Our emotions will not control us; instead, we will have joy in our hearts. Our minds and our bodies will be at peace (v. 9).

God, today I choose to set my mind on you, believing in your goodness and your authority over everything that happens in my life. Help me not to waver in my belief nor to let my emotions take control of my mind and body.

WORTHY OF OBEDIENCE

They are a warning to your servant,
a great reward for those who obey them.
PSALM 19:11 NLT

Obedience gets a bad rap. As children we struggle to obey the authority of our parents. As adults we struggle with government and bosses. We like to be in control of the decisions we make. When we read the Word and discover that we are supposed to obey it, our independent, autonomous minds immediately think "Whoa there! Why should I?"

Here is why: God is worthy of our obedience. He is worth dying to ourselves and saying no to our wrongful desires. Not only will our obedience result in his pleasure, but it will result in *good* things for us. He honors and blesses the obedient heart that is willing to deny its own wants and follow his instruction. We edify God through our obedience which will pour forth from a heart that loves the Lord. He will reward it!

God, give me a heart that longs to obey you. I am still so self-focused and willing to deny your ways for something I want. Forgive me for my unwillingness and help me obey you simply because you are worthy of it!

ESTABLISHED IN TRUTH

"I do not ask that you take them out of the world, but that you keep them from the evil one. They are not of the world, just as I am not of the world. Sanctify them in the truth; your word is truth. As you sent me into the world, so I have sent them into the world."

JOHN 17:15-18 ESV

Jesus made it clear that we, as his followers, are living in a world that is not our home. There are troubles, we suffer, the enemy is busy being an enemy, and the sin nature is against us as we pursue holiness. But despite these difficulties, we are set apart, established in the truth, and always pushing against the forces of darkness that wage war against our souls.

When we fail to study or understand the Word, we miss out on living by its power. We become indistinguishable from the rest of the world. We begin to look like those around us in the way we absorb the influences of the world. When we make the Word part of our daily lives, we influence others with a knowledge of God and a passion for living in sanctity just as Christ prayed for us. Are we grounding ourselves in the truth so as to withstand the attacks of the enemy and the influence of the world?

God, thank you for your Word—your Word is truth. Help me to establish my heart and mind in it so I am prepared to walk in holiness and not cave to the sway of the world.

ORDAINED BY MERCY

Praise the LORD!
Oh give thanks to the LORD, for he is good;
for his mercy is everlasting.
PSALM 106:1 NASB

What weighs heavy on your mind today? Have you come up against an unseen trial? Has trouble arisen in relationships, work, or home? When unexpected difficulties enter your life, it helps to repeat this phrase: "This has been ordained by boundless love and mercy."

God is Jehovah El Roi, "the God who sees." His eyes are on you (Psalm 33:18), and your way is directed and supported by his hand (Psalm 37:23-24). Not only does God see and direct your steps, but he is gracious and full of mercy (Psalm 145:8). It is by his mercy that we are not consumed by the terrors of the world (Lamentations 3:22). Everything that comes your way is ordained by the mercy of God which never runs out. Declare his sovereign care over you and whatever hangs heavy on your heart today.

Lord, thank you for seeing me and knowing every part of my life. I know that I can trust you with every challenge because it is your love and mercy that direct my steps. Help me choose to trust you today.

GRACE FOR SAMENESS

"The LORD will guide you continually,
and satisfy your soul in drought,
and strengthen your bones;
you shall be like a watered garden,
and like a spring of water, whose waters do not fail."

ISAIAH 58:11 NKJV

Monday comes, and then Tuesday, and the days and weeks sometimes drag together in the mundane. Too many of the same, plodding days can wear you down and cause you to fall into a rut. When life looks unfulfilling, remember that with Christ you are fulfilled. His grace is for you not only on the days when things go really well or terribly wrong, but also when the days are simply long.

Instead of finding a way to zone out of the monotony of the daily ins and outs, water the garden of your soul. On the days when you most want to get away from it all, dig into the Word and pursue the Lord. Don't lay down your arms in surrender; allow the Lord to lead you deeper into him, to satisfy your soul, and to strengthen your bones. Press in, pray for grace, and be courageous in stamping out your unbelief and the lies of the enemy.

Lord, sometimes I am brought down by the sameness of my days. Help me remain faithful in seeking you, to pursue things that will keep my soul refreshed, and to find your joy spurring me onward.

A DIRECTED HEART

Your word is a lamp to my feet
and a light to my path.
PSALM 119:105 ESV

When you give your heart to Christ, you are surrendering to him your ideals for your life. You're allowing him to take ownership of the minutes, days, and years. You are saying, "I know your ways are higher than my ways" as you continue to learn the art of abandoning your own desires and plans in order to trust those of your Maker.

God really is trustworthy with your life. Everything he does is good, whether or not you can currently see it as such. Today, ask yourself this question: what can I do to demonstrate a heart directed by the Lord? Perhaps you have been struggling to control a situation and God is asking you for a surrendered heart. Maybe you don't understand the difficulties you are facing, and you are desperately searching for peace. Remember that God is faithfully leading you along the path. Your heart, given to him, is in a very safe place. Let him lead it.

God, it is hard to let you be the one to guide my steps. I fear the unknown and desire to control my days. Help me to trust your good plan, and to demonstrate my faith in you today.

DILIGENCE

We want each of you to show this same diligence to the very end, so that what you hope for may be fully realized. We do not want you to become lazy, but to imitate those who through faith and patience inherit what has been promised.

HEBREWS 6:11-12 NIV

Does your life demonstrate to the Lord that you desire growth? Without becoming legalistic in your thoughts of what it means to pursue Christ, can you genuinely say that the way you live and act shows a desire to go deeper into the heart of God?

The author of Hebrews encouraged his readers to be diligent. It's good advice for believers. Be diligent in following Christ and in what he has called you to at this time. Remember that what you hope for will be fully realized in the fulfillment of the promises of God. Press on, so that through faith, perseverance, and patience you will obtain what has been promised. Study your Bible, meet with likeminded believers, pray at all times, go deeply with God. Do your part to show him your love.

Lord, help me to not become lazy in my pursuit of you but to continually be reminded of the joy and privilege it is to know your heart. Holy Spirit, help me to be diligent in the things you have called me to—most of all to love you and love others.

CERTAINTY

Deep in your hearts you know that every promise of the LORD your God has come true. Not a single one has failed!

JOSHUA 23:14 NLT

There aren't many among us who would say they love uncertainty. We like to know what will happen and when; surprises are often unwelcome. In reality though, not much is certain in life. Relationships change. Jobs change. Sometimes even our purpose in life changes.

It is in the middle of the uncertainties and unknown that we need to ask an important question: when has the Lord not known? When has he been surprised with change? And of course, the answer is: never! God has never not known. He has always orchestrated with perfect grace the story of our lives. There are some things that *are* certain in life:

- I am God's child, whom he chose because he delighted in me;
- God loves me, and his love for me has not once diminished; and
- The Lord is yet leading me into good things.

Lord, in the midst of life's surprises I am prone to forget the things that are firmly fixed. Help me cling to the truth rather than dwell on that which I cannot control.

ROOM TO BREATHE

You gave a wide place for my steps under me,
and my feet did not slip.
PSALM 18:36 ESV

If you have ever gone hiking on a mountain or perhaps into a canyon, you know how terrifying it can be to come to a narrow place on the path. Suddenly, seeing the edge near, you become dizzy, short of breath, and sure that you will stumble over the side. It is a great relief when the path once again widens, and you can breathe freely.

Sometimes life seems to be closing in on us, and that edge comes terrifyingly close. But God did not intend for us to live on that narrow edge. Psalm 18 speaks of a wide and spacious place for our steps. The word in Hebrew is *ravach* which means "to breathe freely, to have ample room, to be refreshed." What a beautiful picture of what the Lord does when we feel like life is suffocating us. If you are there today, ask God to bring you into a spacious place so you can experience healing and be reminded of his tender love. You will be refreshed in his Spirit and breathe freely.

Lord, thank you for assuring me that I will not walk forever on the edge. Please lead me into a wide place where I can breathe, find healing, and rest from being too close to the edge.

NO UNFINISHED WORK

There is now no condemnation
for those who are in Christ Jesus.
ROMANS 8:1 NIV

Do you ever get tired of fighting the enemy's lies? Are
you sometimes tempted beyond your strength, and
you start to believe those lies as truth and accept the
condemnation as your lot in life? Sometimes the Lord feels
far from us, and while we know that he never forsakes us,
we have to choose to believe the truth and act on it when
we feel only the weight of sin and condemnation.

The truth is, God will never leave the work unfinished
which is why you can trust him and rejoice in the sorrow
that you face over your sin. God will change you; you will
not always fight as you do now. God will continue to see
Christ when he looks at you. He will not lose patience with
you. He will not leave you to figure out how to conquer
your sin on your own, no matter how many times you mess
up. Stand firm in your fight against the enemy, dear friend.

God, thank you that when you look at me you see Christ
and not my failure. You see your daughter as pure,
blameless, and redeemed from sin. You do not see the
shameful, blemished, or dishonorable person that the
enemy tells me I am. May I choose to believe the truth and
persist in my fight against the enemy's lies.

Faith over Fear

They do not fear bad news;
they confidently trust the Lord to care for them.
They are confident and fearless
and can face their foes triumphantly.
PSALM 112:7-8 NLT

Bad news is unfortunately part of life; there is no way to escape it, and the only thing we can control is our response to the events that rock our boats. Thankfully, as those who fear the Lord and obey his commands, we have assurance of the Lord's care when things are going wrong. Because of this, we don't have to be afraid of bad news, such as losing work, having an illness, or the passing of a loved one. It's not that these things won't happen to us, but we have the promise of the Lord's care when they do happen. Because of this, fear need not rule our hearts. Stress and anxiety over what might happen, or perhaps what is currently happening, need not consume us.

How do you respond to bad news? Does discouragement overwhelm you? Does fear keep you trapped in a cycle of despair? Lift your eyes to God and declare your trust in his care. Confidence and fearlessness are yours in Christ.

God, I declare my trust in you today. I know you care for all of your creation, and you see the trials that I am walking through, too. Help me depend on your goodness instead of succumbing to worry.

NEVER SETTLE

He has satisfied the thirsty soul,
and he has filled the hungry soul with what is good.
PSALM 107:9 NASB

We live in a beautiful world: mountains, lakes, oceans, flowers, sunrises, and sunsets bring us alive with appreciation for such beauty. Beyond nature, human relationships bring great joy to our hearts and cause deep love to pour forth. God was gracious in giving us a wonderful world. He gives us a taste of the beauty and joy that will be ours in eternity.

We must never settle, however, for *good enough*. Earthly pleasures are meant to awaken a longing for Christ and his kingdom but were never meant to satisfy us completely. Ask the Holy Spirit to renew your mind and cause a desire for God to grow in you. What things are you settling for that God would have you lay aside in order to pursue true joy and satisfaction?

Holy Spirit, awaken my longing for the only thing that will truly satisfy my heart. Thank you for this beautiful world, but may I never become so satisfied with it that I forget the real thing. What good have I if I gain the world but lose my soul?

UNSTOPPABLE

I know that you can do all things
and that no plan of yours can be ruined.
JOB 42:2 NCV

Do you really believe that God can do anything? Do you truly believe that his plan will triumph? So much in the world seems to demonstrate that evil is winning; wickedness appears to be prevailing. It is easy to become disheartened when we read the headlines and see the lack of fear of the Lord in this world.

Be assured though—nothing can stop the plan of the Lord. He is the One you can place your confidence in without fear of disappointment. When evil is demonstrated all around you and God seems quiet, when things go against your expectations of how you think God should respond, remember that his plan cannot be ruined. Make sure your heart is established in the Word, and you will not be shaken. "For the Lord watches over the way of the righteous, but the way of the wicked leads to ruin" (Psalm 1:6).

God, I confess that the wickedness of the world causes me to become overwhelmed and to doubt that you are still on your throne and in total control. Help me trust in your plan, which cannot be thwarted.

No Shifting

Whatever is good and perfect is a gift coming down to us from God our Father, who created all the lights in the heavens. He never changes or casts a shifting shadow.

JAMES 1:17 NLT

Have you ever had one of these days? You wake up happy, enthusiastic about life, and ready to take on whatever challenges come your way? But by mid-morning the stresses and irritations of the day have soured your attitude. Try as you might to recover, the zeal is gone, and you are left longing for the end of the day.

Though our moods and emotions shift almost hourly, God remains constantly the same. He is forever loving, good, kind merciful, just, humble, and patient. What a relief that our ever-fluctuating sentiments do not reflect upon his character. We can take some time to thank him for his constancy today and ask the Spirit for the same steadiness of character to be displayed in our own lives.

Lord, I am so glad that you never change! Thank you for being constantly good and full of mercy toward those who love you. I am so undeserving of your grace, but please help me walk in it today, relying on you for strength and not on my circumstances.

PERFECT WEAKNESS

God is faithful, who has called you into fellowship
with his Son, Jesus Christ our LORD.
1 CORINTHIANS 1:9 NIV

Friend, you need to hear this: the Christian walk will
never truly be easy, so stop hoping for ease. Honestly,
how amazing is it when God shows his faithfulness in the
difficult and desperate situations? It's much more riveting
than when you handle something all on your own! His
power is made perfect in your weakness, and the added
bonus is that it gives him glory. It is his grace that allows
you to feel your weakness and trust in his faithfulness.

What part of your life do you need to surrender to him
today? What weakness do you need to thank him for?
What challenge do you need to embrace as a gift? He does
not waste the hurts that you endure, and he will not see
you depend solely on yourself. He is too good, too faithful,
and too desirous of your praise to let you get by in life on
your own strength.

God, while I would prefer the strength to be able to
handle hard situations on my own, I am thankful that you
know that is not the best thing for me! May my weakness
and these challenges cause me to depend fully on you
and give glory to you alone.

He Hears

In my trouble I called to the LORD.
I cried out to my God for help.
From his temple he heard my voice;
my call for help reached his ears.

PSALM 18:6 NCV

Few of us cry to the Lord from the same place that David did when he wrote this psalm. We probably are not fleeing from an evil king who is seeking to destroy us. David experienced rescue in the truest sense of the word—he really was *that close* to death.

Our cries may not be for physical rescue, but they are no less desperate. We find ourselves struggling in a relationship that causes deep pain. We experience sickness, poverty, or longing for a child which our body cannot conceive. Whatever our struggles are today, they are no less important to God than David's need to be rescued from the hands of his enemy. God will hear our cries to him in our troubles. Our calls do not fall on deaf ears, and our needs are not insignificant to him. He is not content to watch our suffering but will come to our aid. We can cry out to him today. We can let our voices be heard! He will hear, and he will be our support (Psalm 18:18)

God, thank you for hearing my cries when I am in trouble, for caring about the things that weigh on my heart. Come to me today; rescue me because you delight in me.

CONTENTMENT IN TODAY

This is the day the LORD has made;
we will rejoice and be glad in it.
PSALM 118:24 NKJV

Anticipation can encourage our hearts to persevere through dry seasons, looking forward to the good things to come. But it can also become all-consuming as we anticipate something so much that we are distracted from what God has for us today. If we find ourselves longing for a time or situation in life that is different from what we have now, we need to pursue contentment in God's place for this moment, today.

What does being present and content in today mean? For some of us, it is giving thanks for our small, comfortable home. It can also be the strength we feel to diligently work hard as needed. Maybe we are able to love and encourage ourselves and others through sadness and exhaustion because the Lord delivers grace. Maybe we have peace whether we are experiencing sickness or health. Maybe we feel God's heart of love for people who are separated from him for a time. Today has new mercies and God's love is unfailing. Today is good.

Lord, you have given me today, and it is good. Help me be mindful of the ways in which I can give you glory by finding contentment in my present circumstances.

DELIGHT OF THE WORD

The precepts of the LORD are right,
giving joy to the heart.
The commands of the LORD are radiant,
giving light to the eyes.

PSALM 19:8 NIV

Have you ever had the pleasure of reading a book that captivated you so much that you neglected your responsibilities? A well-written story is a gift to anyone who loves to read. The Bible was not written with the intention of making it impossible to put down. And let's be honest. Sometimes we struggle to keep our focus when we are reading through the Old Testament laws and genealogies. But those parts of the Word are also a source of joy and inspiration to us when we study and learn the back stories and the contexts.

When we diligently give time to learning the Word and not just reading a passage of Scripture and then moving on with our day, we find a whole wealth of information that causes us to be enthralled with God and the gift of his Word. It is a source of joy for the heart and a delight to the eyes.

God, thank you for the gift of your Word. I know there is so much treasure to uncover, so help me be diligent in studying it.

WHEN YOU NEED IT

Come boldly to the throne of our gracious God.
There we will receive his mercy, and we will find grace
to help us when we need it most.

HEBREWS 4:16 NLT

It's very likely that you will be confronted by your
weakness today. Whether displayed as a weakness in your
body, or a weakness in your ability to overcome sin, or a
weakness in finding yourself up against something you
don't know how to master, every day you are challenged
by your weakened natural self.

The good news is that God's grace doesn't leave you to
power through on your own. In your exhaustion, there
is grace to endure through a long day. In your mistakes,
there is grace that forgives the repentant heart. In your
obstacles, there is grace to remind you that God is helping
you through even the most impossible of situations. Lean
into that grace. Come boldly to the throne and request it.
It's yours for the taking.

God, you are so gracious. Thank you for the grace that you
pour out on me on the days when I am so challenged by
my own weakness. Thank you that I need not find a way
to push through on my own. May your grace carry me
through today.

END IN SIGHT

Why are you cast down, O my soul,
and why are you in turmoil within me?
Hope in God; for I shall again praise him,
my salvation and my God.

PSALM 43:5 ESV

Sometimes life is seasoned with sadness. It colors our days, nullifies normally joyful events, and weighs us down. When we are walking through grief, we can remember that the Lord tasted the pain of grief, too, and he can sympathize with our struggles. Anguish is an unfortunate part of life, but as believers we have the hope of an end to sorrow.

If we are facing sorrow or pain right now, we must remember that it will not last forever. God will bring restoration, even if it's in eternity. Sorrow may last for the night, but joy comes with the morning (Psalm 30:5). God is the lifter of our heads (Psalm 3:3). He will wipe every tear from our eyes (Revelation 21:4). These promises in Scripture are reminders that God is well aware of our pain and has every intention to completely do away with it. Take heart, my friend. The night will come to an end.

God, sometimes the sorrows in life are almost too much to bear. When I feel myself sliding into despair, help me raise my eyes to heaven. I know you see me, and you know my sorrow. Lift my head, Lord Jesus.

ALL HIS WAYS

All the ways of the LORD are loving and faithful
toward those who keep the demands of his covenant.
PSALM 25:10 NIV

Read that verse again and take note of the first few words.
For those of us who have decided to spend our lives
pursuing the righteousness of Christ, all the ways of the
Lord are loving and faithful. Not some of them. Not the
ones we agree with or can get behind. Not the ones other
people recognize as beneficial for our lives. Not the ones
that are comfortable or convenient. All of them.

Do our lives reflect the belief that all of God's ways are
loving and faithful? Or are our tendencies like those of
the Israelites in the wilderness? They tended toward
complaining and wishing their lives were different. Are
we like that, trying to make things happen the way we
want because we're discontented with our perception
of the Lord's will? When we accept in faith that God sits
enthroned in the heavens and has plans to direct our lives
with love and faithfulness, peace will adorn our hearts and
minds. Do we trust him today?

God, thank you that I can trust all your ways, even when
they don't make sense to me. What peace it brings me to
know that it is perfect love and faithfulness that guide my
every step.

TRUTH

Do you presume on the riches of his kindness and forbearance and patience, not knowing that God's kindness is meant to lead you to repentance?

ROMANS 2:4 ESV

There is something every believer needs to know with absolute certainty: God's truth is kind. It is not condemning, defeating, or cutting. If you are hearing anything that feels like that, you need to recognize it as a lie from Satan. God's truth is full of mercy and kindness. It is life-giving. This doesn't mean that you will not be challenged by it; the Word is alive and active and is meant to reveal to us the state of your heart before God. But what you should not receive from the Word is anything that causes you to believe the idea that you will never measure up nor find victory. You are believing the lie if you think that you are unloved.

Friend, God's kindness, patience, and love pours forth from his heart so that we will recognize our need for repentance, turn from our sin, and find life in his ways. We may feel sorrow over our sin—and that is good. We may struggle to believe that we will overcome our sin—and that is okay. Accept the truth and refute the lies.

Lord, your kindness humbles me. Thank you for being so gracious in dealing with my sin. Help me refute the lies of the enemy and stand firm in your truth.

BLAMELESS AND HAPPY

Happy are those who live pure lives,
who follow the LORD's teachings.
PSALM 119:1 NCV

One of the promises of Scripture that brings the greatest hope to the life of a believer is this one: following God's instructions does not lead to an arduous and uninteresting life, but to complete happiness! His commands are given for our joy because living according to them leads to a life that is blameless and brings greater pleasure than anything the world can offer.

Doing what is right in God's eyes may not always mean that we are accepted or approved by others, but we have the knowledge of a pure heart before the Lord which is far better than the approval of man. Walking blamelessly will bring greater satisfaction to our lives than anything known to those who do not follow the Lord. Press on in the pursuit of purity, friend. It will not go unrewarded.

God, I am so thankful that your ways have been made known to me—that I do not have to wonder about the right way to live. Help me give myself to following your ways fully, that I may press on toward the goal to win the prize for which God called me heavenward in Christ Jesus (Philippians 3:14).

MAY

Eat honey, for it is good,
and the drippings
of the honeycomb
are sweet to your taste.

PROVERBS 24:13 ESV

GRACIOUS ACCEPTANCE

If God is for us,
who can be against us?
ROMANS 8:31 NIV

The astounding thing about Christianity is this wild idea that the all-powerful, completely holy, faultless God, chose to bring sin-ridden, selfish people into his family. He didn't say, "Okay, I guess you can hang out, but try not to do anything stupid." He made us his children, and as such, he is completely one hundred percent on our side. That undeserved, over-the-top grace should blow our minds.

Every single day we fail, and yet every single day God tells us, "I love you and I forgive you." He doesn't keep us at arm's length, but rather he welcomes us home, gives us good gifts, and promises to be a safe place for us. Let yourself respond to his grace in your life today. Praise him for his mercy that called you out of darkness and into his light. Praise him that he pours out his favor on you every single day. Praise him for being your strength and your shield.

God, I am in awe of your favor. Thank you for lavishing it on me daily and in so many ways. Open my eyes, that I may recognize your grace, and have the capacity to extend it to the people in my own life.

PRAISE FOR THE ORDINARY

You, O LORD, are my hope,
my trust, O LORD, from my youth.
Upon you I have leaned from before my birth;
you are he who took me from my mother's womb.
My praise is continually of you.
PSALM 71:5-6 ESV

Ordinary life can sometimes be the hardest to walk with a joyful attitude. When we are neither on the mountaintops nor in the valleys, when life is neither thrilling nor painful, we level out to a place where we're either pressing in for the Lord's perseverance or forgetting God's blessings (Psalm 103:2). It is during these mundane days that we need to continue to acknowledge the Lord's sovereign goodness and respond faithfully to his character.

God is with us through every single day of our lives. He walks with us atop the mountains of joy, through the dark valleys of sorrow, and everywhere in between. What else would be an appropriate response other than to continually praise him? Acknowledge his faithfulness. Thank him for his grace. Do not allow growth to be stunted by the commonplace days in life.

Lord, thank you for your faithfulness through every day of my life. Help me to praise you in every situation, and not be brought down by the ordinariness of life.

Never Wasted Time

I rise before dawn and cry for help;
I have put my hope in your word.
PSALM 119:147 NIV

Perhaps your mind comes alive as darkness settles. Or perhaps you rise with the sun and find motivation during the peaceful moments before your house awakens. Some people experience and love both times in their lives. In the different seasons of life, our times with the Lord also change. You may not have hours available to you to read, journal, and pray before your day gets going, and that's okay. But be encouraged to make time in your day—in the morning, noon, or night—to do as David did and cry for help.

We weren't meant to move through our days on our own; the Holy Spirit and the Word of God were given as gifts to us to help us from end to end. Do you seek help from these sources? Or do you try to power through the day on your own, thinking that you can spend your time more wisely than "crying for help?" Find the time of day that works best for you to be with the Lord and don't neglect it. It is never wasted time.

God, I tend to think that I can spend my time most wisely by filling it with as many productive things as possible. Help me remember that the most important thing I can do is give my time to you.

ARMED AND READY

Strengthen yourselves so that you will live here on earth
doing what God wants, not the evil things people want.

1 PETER 4:2 NCV

It is interesting to think that Jesus, while on earth,
encountered all of the inconveniences and irritations that
we now experience, and he overcame them without sin.
Never did he lose his temper with his annoying friends.
Never did he complain about the lack of sleep. Never did
he justify letting a bad attitude settle into his heart.

Our charge is to have the same attitude Christ did while
he walked the earth. If our attitudes are no better than
our circumstances, we can expect life to be miserable.
The world will tell us that a sour attitude is justified—
when things are going badly, what is a person to do? But
we know the truth: we have the grace of God to walk in
righteousness regardless of the situation, we have the Spirit
of God empowering us to make good choices. When we
arm ourselves with these things today, we overcome with a
Christ-like attitude all the troubles that come our way.

Lord, thank you for sustaining me with your Spirit and with
grace, that I might choose to worship and live righteously
today. May my attitude today reflect a thankful heart.

EVERYDAY MIRACLES

Come and see what our God has done,
what awesome miracles he performs for people!
PSALM 66:5 NLT

Sometimes we need to be reminded that God's potential is limitless. Sure, we read the stories in the Old Testament about the plagues and the rescue of the Israelites from exile; we read about Jesus turning water into wine and raising people from the dead. But does that mean much for us today? We seem to find ourselves in a similar situation as the Jews did in the Roman Empire—oppressed and hoping for God to swoop in and rescue us.

It takes a lot of faith to wait and hope that God will bring justice like he promised he will. We may not see his return in our lifetimes, but will we choose to see his power displayed in the small, daily things? Will we choose to acknowledge his protection over us? Do we acknowledge his provision of all we need? Are we open to his power to woo hearts back to himself? These are powerful miracles, too. We praise God for the way his power is shown in our day-to-day lives!

God, I admit that sometimes I'm looking for you to show up in a big, astounding way. Help me to remember that your sustenance of my life is a miracle. Help me to give praise for all the awesome things you do.

LEVEL GROUND

As for me, I shall walk in my integrity;
redeem me, and be gracious to me.
My foot stands on level ground;
in the great assembly I will bless the LORD.
PSALM 26:11-12 ESV

The imagery in the Psalms is a great tool for the imagination. Picture yourself the object of the persecution: friends, coworkers, or even your family members taunt you for your faithfulness to the Lord and the way you choose to obey him. Imagine you are ridiculed for your beliefs and under constant scrutiny. Your persecutors are just waiting for you to trip up so they can have more ammo to fire at you.

And yet, you stand on level ground. You know the truth of who you are in Christ and what he says about you. You know the end of the story, and therefore you have faith. You know that because of your integrity and because of the Lord's grace, you will be redeemed from the fire. It is from this place of knowing the solid foundation upon which you stand that you can worship, declaring the Lord's goodness, keeping your eyes on him instead of on your troubles. Plant your feet firmly in Christ, and you will not be moved.

God, thank you for being my sure foundation, my source of steadfastness. Help me remain steadied on you through worship, even in the midst of life's difficulties.

PLEASING VERSUS TRUSTING

Without faith it is impossible to please God, because anyone who comes to him must believe that he exists and that he rewards those who earnestly seek him.

HEBREWS 11:6 NIV

We all want to be found pleasing; we love to know that we are enjoyed, treasured, and beautiful. In our relationships with people, we do what we think will make others happy and like us more. Failure on our part to perform can cause us to be insecure and afraid that we will lose their love. If we are not careful, we can take this same mindset into our relationship with God; but seeking to please him and trusting him are two different things. Trying to please relies on us doing something, rather than relying on God's character to remain constant in love toward us regardless of our actions.

Do not put your worth in your ability to please God by performing well. Trust that he loves you and will respond with mercy toward you even when you're not at your best. Trust his character instead of being consumed by your failure. As you trust him, you will be delightful to him.

God, thank you that your love is not dependent upon my performance. May I be found pleasing to you, not because of what I do, but because I have chosen to trust who you say you are.

THE PERFECT WAY

God arms me with strength,
and he makes my way perfect.

PSALM 18:32 NLT

If today turns out differently than we planned or hoped for, it shows good biblical intentions to remain committed to God's will for our lives. Our plans are just that—*our* plans. We think we know what is best for us and for our day, but in reality, we are sinful, selfish beings and our choices for our lives will never be up to the standard that Christ sets for us.

God's ways are always perfect. You may not understand his plans for you, but they are good. Ask God to arm you with strength today so that you can graciously accept his ways rather than your own. With God as your guide, Jesus as your strength, and the Holy Spirit as your helper, you can do all things!

God, thank you that your ways are always best. Help me today to trust your plans even though they may be different than what I hope for myself. Let me not hold tightly to things that will not serve me well, but rather, strengthen me to demonstrate a heart surrendered to you.

NEARNESS VERSUS NUMBNESS

The nearness of God is good for me;
I have made the LORD God my refuge,
so that I may tell of all your works.

PSALM 73:28 NASB

What do you turn to when things go wrong? Do you rage-clean the house? Do you default to zoning out on social media? Maybe your choice is to lose yourself in a Netflix series or a book? Our human tendency is to find a distraction from our pain and disappointment, numbing ourselves from the reality until our disappointment or frustration subsides. But what if that isn't what God intends for us to do?

What if, instead of finding a diversion from our disappointment, we embraced it and took it to Jesus? What if we did like the psalmist did and made God our refuge rather than these other things? We can speak the truth to ourselves, saying "If all is lost, God's nearness is good. I have all I need because he is my refuge." We can let him take the place of these other things when disappointment finds us.

Lord, forgive me for filling my space and time with things to numb my pain, rather than turning to you. Your nearness is my good; thank you that I can find a safe place in you at any time.

STRONGHOLD

The LORD is my light and my salvation;
whom shall I fear?
The LORD is the stronghold of my life;
of whom shall I be afraid?
PSALM 27:1 ESV

We all have fears: fear of losing a loved one, fear of not being able to provide for our families, fear of illness or injury, fear of being forced into situations that make us uncomfortable. Fear, if we allow it, will control us. When we are controlled by fear, we tend to make decisions based on that dangerous emotion, or we avoid certain situations, so we don't need to face what we're afraid of.

David asked the question, "Whom shall I fear?" He recognized God as his stronghold—a formidable place of protection. God cannot be defeated, does not have weaknesses, and will never fall to the enemy. Of course, David would make God his stronghold! Can we say the same about God in our lives? Are we allowing fear to be a stronghold? Consider today how fear affects you and ask the Holy Spirit to enable you to walk in boldness.

God, I don't want to be controlled by fear. Help me know that with you as my God, I have nothing to be afraid of.

APPEAL OF OBEDIENCE

He will cover you with his feathers.
He will shelter you with his wings.
His faithful promises are your armor and protection.
PSALM 91:4 NLT

To the unbeliever, your life might look really good. It might not be that you have nicer things, or that your life is free from problems, but your life will appeal to others who see the blessings of following God as they are manifested in your life. Repeatedly in Scripture we are told that those who obey the Lord's commands are under his protection and will be blessed.

And it is true! So many difficulties are avoided when we simply walk in obedience. It's not that our lives are better than someone else's, or that it is easier when we obey, but so many difficulties are avoided or better solved when we submit to God's ways. Our obedience opens up a spring of blessings that pour forth over our lives, and it really will look good to those who do not have such grace. If we are confronted by someone wondering why things are so good in our lives, we can tell them of the God who shelters us under his wings because we have chosen to obey him.

God, thank you that because I choose to obey, I am guarded by your faithful promises. May I never waver in following steadily after you, and may my life reflect the blessing of knowing and obeying God.

FOCUS ON FORGIVENESS

*Lord, you are kind and forgiving
and have great love for those who call to you.*
PSALM 86:5 NCV

Does your sin weigh on you? If you are struggling to overcome a certain sin, it is easy to feel defeated. Satan would have you believe that God is disappointed with you. But, dear friend, regardless of your mistakes there is no reason to sit around being afraid that God is unhappy with you. You confessed, he saw your heart, and he forgave the offense. You can move on and accept his grace.

You can never improve if you just sit and stare at the problem. Forgive yourself and go forward with his forgiveness empowering you to be better next time. Don't get down on yourself for messing up; God loves the heart that is humble. He is always ready to extend his love to you. Regardless of what you experience in the world, God's kindness is not like human kindness. His forgiveness is not like human forgiveness. His love is not like human love. It is unconditional, abounding, and always faithful. Let that knowledge encourage you to press on past the disappointment in yourself and the lies of the enemy.

God, your kindness and forgiveness humble me. Help me keep my focus on your constant love rather than my struggles.

RELIABLE AND RIGHTEOUS

The fear of the LORD is pure,
enduring forever.
The decrees of the LORD are firm,
and all of them are righteous.

PSALM 19:9 NIV

In today's world of scams and phishing it is difficult to trust. We want reliable information, but it is hard to know what or who we can believe. How comforting it is, then, to know that there is no false information in the Word of God. We can trust that the eternal truth available to us in the Bible is fully reliable, and that every word spoken is trustworthy. We can believe that every promise will be fulfilled.

If we are struggling with the misinformation in the world today, we can feed ourselves less of it. Instead, we can get into the Word and fill our minds with that which is pure, true, and lovely. The added bonus is that we will also be able to better discern whatever is false once we know the truth. Give thanks today that we can read the Word without wondering if any of it is a scam.

God, thank you that your Word is reliable and righteous. How good it is to know that I can read it without any concern of being tricked. Help me fill my mind with what is true so that I can discern what is false in the world.

STRONG AND COURAGEOUS

"Be strong and courageous. Do not be frightened, and
do not be dismayed, for the LORD your God is with you
wherever you go."
JOSHUA 1:9 ESV

Do you find yourself encountering a daunting situation
today? Maybe you are facing changes in your job, an
unexpected move, or challenges in a relationship. God's
people have come up against difficult situations for
generations, but he has always made it clear that their
challenges were not theirs alone; God was with them!

Do you think the Lord told Joshua to be strong and
courageous because the journey ahead of him was going
to be simple, easy, or restful? No! The Lord knew that
what lay ahead of Joshua would be very difficult, and that
without courage he would not succeed. But his command
to be strong and courageous came with a beautiful
promise: "for the Lord your God is with you wherever you
go." Just as the Lord was with Joshua, the Lord is with
you in this current situation. Friend, be strong and very
courageous, for the Lord your God is with you!

Lord, the promise of your presence brings me comfort. Help
me cling to your presence as I face my challenges today,
especially as I know that I am not facing them alone. Give
me courage to move forward, keeping my eyes on you!

DEFINED BY MERCY

Do not remember the rebellious sins of my youth.
Remember me in the light of your unfailing love,
for you are merciful, O LORD.

PSALM 25:7 NLT

Our history can haunt us. Many of us would probably
admit to choices which we made in the past are now
regretted, and we wish that we had walked in obedience to
the Lord then. Instead, we chose our own path. We might
let our past define us or spend our days trying to forget
who we were, running as far from that person as we can.

But God never sees us as someone who needs
redefinition. He sees us covered in mercy from the
moment we turn to him. We do not need to make
ourselves clean in order for him to love us. Remember the
story of the adulteress in John 8? Check out the beginning
of the chapter up to verse eleven. It's a good read! Jesus
did not define her by her sin; he simply spoke mercy over
her. We can grab hold of that mercy for our own lives. We
do not define ourselves by our pasts. We simply walk in
obedience today.

Lord, your mercy humbles me. How good you are to see
me—not branded by my sin but covered in your love.
Help me to take hold of your mercy and forgiveness and
walk in obedience to you today.

FRENZY FOR FREEDOM

The peace of God, which surpasses all comprehension,
will guard your hearts and minds in Christ Jesus.

PHILIPPIANS 4:7 NASB

Do you find yourself doing too much these days? It is
easy to overcommit with activities, work and church
obligations, and volunteer opportunities; the list goes
on. In the midst of it all, you must make sure that you are
giving yourself time with the source of life and peace.
Pushing through a busy season only works so well, but
if you give yourself time to worship, you will endure so
much better.

When you give yourself to prayer and thanksgiving, you
will find the peace of God. Do not speak burn out over
yourself. Go before the Lord with your burdens and
give him your time. Remember, when you seek first his
kingdom and his righteousness, all these other things
will be added unto you. Overcommitted or not, weary of
the grind or not, find yourself first at the feet of Jesus and
everything else will fall into place.

God, you know how easy it is for me to fill my time and
mind until I am overwhelmed. Help me first to seek you
before loading myself up with all the things I "must do."
Your peace will surround me as I give myself to you.

LOOKING AT HIS LOVE

For your steadfast love is before my eyes,
and I walk in your faithfulness.
PSALM 26:3 ESV

If life has become chaotic and your relationship with
the Lord needs some nurturing, think about this phrase
from Psalm 26—his steadfast love is before your eyes. If
you have been walking with the Lord for a long time, it is
easy to fall into a ho-hum routine with God. It's easy over
time to turn your attention to him only when you need
something or when things go wrong.

When we forget what the Lord's love really means and
what it has done for us, our relationships with God can
become dull. But when we consciously set our minds
on God's love, how we have done nothing to earn that
acceptance, and how his grace is bestowed on us, our own
love is renewed. We can consider the ways the Lord has
shown his love to us recently. We can list them out and
give thanks for his abundant love. It is not lacking.

Lord, forgive me for failing to see the ways that you have
bestowed your love upon me. Help me to see your love
as it is—an amazing gift which I have done nothing to
deserve. May I keep your love before my eyes.

ACTING ON FAITH

My God, my God, why have you abandoned me?
You seem far from saving me,
far away from my groans.
PSALM 22:1 NCV

It is a feeling that we hope to never experience but most of us will at some point in our walk with God. We need to find some sort of understanding when we sense that we have been abandoned or left alone to figure out a situation. Regardless of the specific circumstances, we all have times when God is silent, almost like he has left the room. Our cries are not answered. Our heavy hearts are not comforted. We feel lost.

In these moments, it is important to recognize two truths. First, God has never really left any of us who love him just because we do not sense his presence. Sometimes his quietness is purposeful in leading us to admit to our weaknesses, compelling us to return to a healthy dependency upon him. Second, God's character does not change when we feel forsaken. We are still called to respond faithfully to that character, acting on the knowledge of who he is instead of acting on our emotions. Our God will *never* leave us. That is a promise.

God, in the moments when I don't feel your presence and can't recognize your love, help me act in faith upon the knowledge of who you are.

OVERFLOWING JOY

"I have told you these things so that you will be
filled with my joy. Yes, your joy will overflow!"
JOHN 15:11 NLT

If your circumstances today are less than ideal and you
find yourself tempted to be discouraged which is leading
you to complain, then this devotion is for you. Jesus faced
challenging circumstances during his earthly life. What
was his response when things were going all wrong?
He would go to the Father, spending time in prayer
and supplication to the will of his Father. Jesus spoke of
the importance of remaining in submission to God. It's
important to allow yourself to be pruned of anything that
is not "bearing fruit." It's important to lean into obedience
to his commands.

Why? So that your joy will overflow! If you are facing
challenges today and finding a complaining spirit in
yourself because of it, bring it to the Father so he can
"prune" you and you can be restored to a correct mindset
and to joy!

Lord, when I am tempted to grumble and complain about
the things that are going wrong in my life, remind me to
come to you. You shared all I need to know so that I can
walk in faithfulness and in joy all my days. You are good all
the time.

HOLDING LOOSELY

Let no one who waits on you be ashamed;
Let those be ashamed who
deal treacherously without cause.
PSALM 25:3 NKJV

It is something we will need to be reminded of again and again until the Lord takes us home. Those who surrender their plans to God and allow him complete control of their lives will, as the psalmist puts it, never be ashamed. This includes all things, from the smallest issue, such as the day not starting the way we hoped, to the greatest tragedy, such as losing a job and needing to start over.

If we wait on God, living our lives with hands holding loosely to our hopes and dreams, we will be blessed. Our willingness to surrender will result in honor and peace. On the contrary, those who hold tightly to their plans and are unwilling to compromise, or they disobey God in order fulfill them, will find themselves disgraced. What are you struggling with in order to release your plans to God? Relax your grasp on the way you think things should be, and you will not be ashamed.

Lord, it can be so hard to let go of my expectations for my life. Forgive me for holding so tightly to my plans that I am willing to go against what you say is good and right. May I learn to surrender everything to you.

GENTLE LEADER

He tends his flock like a shepherd:
he gathers the lambs in his arms
and carries them close to his heart;
he gently leads those that have young.

ISAIAH 40:11 NIV

Mandy was angry with God. She had worked so long for something amazing, and it had just been swept out from under her feet. She had no one to blame but God, so blame God she did. For weeks afterwards all she spoke of was her loss. She pointed bitter fingers at her God who had so cruelly stolen a dream from her.

If God were silent on the matter, it would not have mattered. Mandy's heart was too calloused to hear him speak anyway. But in time as the sting of her loss slowly healed, she softened. As she opened her heart to the Lord once again, she realized with great humility that the One whom she had been pointing fingers at was graciously and gently carrying her the whole time. She finally understood why the Lord took her dream away. When we blame God, he doesn't respond in anger but in gentleness, so we can see our flaws, his perfection, and then, finally, his mercy covering them.

God, forgive me for looking past your perfection and seeing only my pain. Let me not become bitter; may your Spirit keep me tender toward you always.

UNDEFEATED

He protects our lives
and does not let us be defeated.
PSALM 66:9 NCV

It's human nature, or the sin nature, to notice the things that go wrong. It's that same nature within us that causes us to see first and foremost the disappointments, discouragements, and problems in our lives. How would our attitudes change if we were aware of all the times that the Lord protects us? If we could see when he does not allow the enemy to attack, or when his hand saves us from physical harm, how would our hearts respond?

A good challenge for today is to live as if we could see all the ways that God is not allowing us to be defeated. We can spend the day giving thanks to God as he acts as Elohim Shomri—our protector—even when we are completely unaware. He who watches over you neither slumbers nor sleeps (Psalm 121:4).

God, how good you are to act as my protector at all times, even when I am completely unaware. Help me to live faithfully today and to not just see all that is going wrong, but to know that you are watching over me and not allowing me to be defeated!

Beautiful Things

Seek the LORD and his strength;
Seek his face continually.
1 CHRONICLES 16:11 NASB

Creating beautiful things requires effort and perseverance, and sometimes it involves disappointment. Think about the things in our lives for which this is true: relationships, gardens, personal growth, or crafting and designing. Our relationships with the Lord also require effort and perseverance, and we will sometimes feel disappointed. If we give up when the going gets tough or when we are overwhelmed with that disappointment, then we will never reap the benefits of the effort and the perseverance—the beautiful, trusting relationship with the Creator himself, refined by fire and able to withstand the pressures.

Think about your relationship with the Lord today. Can you identify the times you have leaned into his strength during some difficulty, then emerged more in love with him? Or is your relationship marked by times when you pulled back, failing to seek God because it was too much? Determine today to seek him no matter what you are facing; create something beautiful with God.

Lord, help me be willing to put in the work it takes into having a beautiful relationship with you. Forgive me for the times I have given up and neglected you because it took more out of me than I wanted to invest. You are worth it!

LAWS

I am overwhelmed with indignation,
for my enemies have disregarded your words.

PSALM 119:139 NLT

Here is a serious question to consider: is there some righteous anger in us when people break God's laws, or do we get angry because people break our laws? God's laws are holy, and we should be filled with righteous anger when we see them neglected or blatantly transgressed. But is that really what makes us angry?

Most of us would admit that we feel more anger over our own laws being broken rather than God's. We get angry when people go against our spoken or unspoken rules, especially when they inconvenience us, irritate us, or mess up our plans. We need to check our hearts today. Is our anger righteous and justified because we desire to see God's laws obeyed? Or do we need to repent of caring more about our own so-called laws?

God, forgive me for giving more value to my own laws than yours. I confess that when I am put out of my way it angers me more than seeing your laws broken. Help me to have the right perspective, and to be slow to anger when I am inconvenienced.

CONFIDENCE

If an army surrounds me,
I will not be afraid.
If war breaks out,
I will trust the LORD.

PSALM 27:3 NCV

Where is your confidence placed today? Do you see today going well because of your own abilities, strengths, and gifts? Some days we get caught up in our own capacity to do things well. We feel strong, capable, and confident. Confidence is not a bad thing itself, but it does need to be properly placed. What would happen if all those things that you trust in were to be stripped away suddenly? Would you still be able to speak with the same confidence that David did in today's verse from Psalms—that though all these horrible and challenging things surround you, you are still confident and unafraid?

David could speak that way, not because he was the toughest guy in the room or had all the things figured out, but because his confidence was in God. He knew that no matter what came at him, he was under the care of the One who held the world in his hands. Place your confidence in God today.

Lord, I admit that sometimes I think I can do everything in my own power. Help me place my confidence in you and not in my own abilities.

QUIET COURAGE

Be strong, and let your heart take courage,
all you who wait for the Lord!
PSALM 31:24 ESV

What does courage look like for you today? Is it loud, adventurous, and enticing? Does it receive applause and affirmation? Or for you, is courage quieter? Perhaps it is waking in the middle of the night to comfort a child or showing up at your job when you are tired and feeling poorly. Are you courageously caring for your sick parents every day? Maybe courage for you is faithfulness through all the challenges, failing to grow weary in doing good.

We have seasons of courage that the world approves of, and we have seasons when only God sees our courage. The quieter seasons are no less important, and God is no less with us through them. Find your strength in him, therefore, in the days when courage is marked by faithfulness. His grace will sustain you.

Lord, it is easy to grow weary in doing good when "doing good" repeats itself with no end in sight. Help me remain faithful to you and to the tasks which you have given me. May I not lose heart, and may your grace give me the power I need to press on.

HOPE FOR YOUR SOUL

The eye of the LORD is on those who fear him,
on those who hope in his mercy,
to deliver their soul from death,
and to keep them alive in famine.

PSALM 33:18-19 NKJV

The world offers so many false sources of hope: job security, the newest technology, or healthier food. The popular message is that if we work hard enough and have the right things, trouble can't touch us. For those who follow Christ, we know that couldn't be further from the truth. Hope isn't found in what we own or who we work for. It is found in the mercy of Christ and in his power to save us from what we really need salvation from—sin and death.

We need to be cautious of the temptation to build up for ourselves "ways of escape" from the troubles that afflict us here on earth. We can depend instead upon the Lord who has the power to deliver us from trouble in this world *and* from eternal destruction. We serve the one who will not allow his faithful ones to see decay (Psalm 16:10). Our hope is safe in him.

Jesus, thank you that I can trust your mercy to save me, not just from the afflictions of this world, but from death itself! May I never turn aside to other things when you offer true hope for my soul.

ABUNDANCE

You have put more joy in my heart
than they have when their grain and wine abound.
PSALM 4:7 ESV

Sometimes "grain and wine" abound in our lives; we
live comfortably with all we need, and perhaps even an
abundance of good gifts. We have joy both in the Lord and
in the blessings that he has bestowed upon us. And then
sometimes God blesses us with that same joy even when
those good things are stripped from us.

Whether we find ourselves in want today or we have an
abundance of blessings, our challenge today is to honor
the giver, not the gifts. We may have beautiful homes, so
we honor the Lord who has provided them for us. We may
have just lost everything, and we honor the Lord who will
yet provide for us through all circumstances. When our joy
is found in Christ, the grain and wine are just the cherries
on top of a beautiful life of true abundance.

Lord, you are so good to me. May I never be so distracted
by the blessings that I forget to honor the one who has
been so gracious. Help my joy be found in you so I can
give praise with much or with little.

GIVING YOUR BEST

For even the Son of Man did not come to be served,
but to serve, and to give his life as a ransom for many.
MARK 10:45 NASB

The humility and kindness of Christ showed up in many
ways during his life on earth, but his attitude of service just
might be the most extraordinary. Jesus did not consider
himself entitled to anything, even though if there was
anyone who ever deserved good, it was him. Instead of
demanding the best for himself, he gave the best of himself.

If we walk in his ways, that should be our goal as well.
Consider how much "heaven" you can give the people in
your life today. In other words, love your opportunities to
gift people with love and kindness the way Jesus would
have done. Take joy in serving and in giving your very best
to others without the need for reciprocation. Pray for eyes
that see opportunities for serving and not how you can
have the best. How can you give the best? Jesus will give
you the grace to see and do his service.

Jesus, I so desire to be like you. Help me see ways to sacrifice
myself for others in a beautiful reflection of you. Show me
the ways that you would show kindness. May I take joy in
giving my best so you can be glorified through me.

REST WITH GOD

Let all that I am wait quietly before God,
for my hope is in him.
PSALM 62:5 NLT

Many of us struggle to rest and to quiet our hearts, minds, and bodies because something might go undone. In the world today we wear busyness like a badge of honor, forgetting that God himself rested. In doing so, God showed us the best way to accomplish good things.

Psalm 127 says that unless the Lord builds the house, those who build it are laboring in vain. In other words, if all of our busyness shows only our unwillingness to relinquish control over a situation, then it will all prove to be for nothing. At the very least the work will not result in the way we were hoping. God commanded rest for mankind, and it is a blessing for us to admit our finite power. We are not able to control every situation, so we need to surrender our goals to God. We can do so now and wait quietly before him today.

Lord, I admit that I try to do all things myself because I want to ensure they are done my way. I am not surrendered to you and your ways when I do that. Please help me step back, rest before you, and trust that things will be best if they are done by you.

GOODNESS AND JUSTICE

The wicked draw the sword and bend the bow
to bring down the poor and needy,
to slay those whose ways are upright.
But their swords will pierce their own hearts,
and their bows will be broken.

PSALM 37:14-15 NIV

It's a question we probably all ask, even those of us who have walked with Christ for a long time. How can a good and loving God allow bad things to happen and evil to flourish? We watch the suffering of innocent people. We see children harmed. We see wicked people do what they want with seemingly no retribution. Doesn't God care? Why doesn't he do something?

It is one of the hardest things that Christians have been called to do—believe in the goodness and justice of God when evil seems to be victorious. But before we decide that we can't take any more of the bad guy winning, let's remember that God sees every evil that is done to the helpless and to his holy ones. He sees and those deeds will not go unpunished. His justice and goodness ensure that all evil will receive its fair retribution. Hold fast, friend.

God, it can be so hard to watch the pain and suffering in this world but help me trust you. My understanding demands justice now, but I know you will bring justice at just the right time.

JUNE

The fear of the LORD is pure,
enduring forever;
the ordinances of the LORD are
reliable and altogether righteous.
They are more desirable than gold—
than an abundance of pure gold;
and sweeter than honey
dripping from a honeycomb.

PSALM 19:9-10 CSB

DISASSEMBLED

Many are the afflictions of the righteous,
but the LORD delivers him out of them all.
PSALM 34:19 ESV

Sometimes for us to love God he needs to take our world apart. We build up our lives with good things, good dreams, and good plans. And then God disassembles it. Why? Because his love cannot have us pursuing things other than him, and his glory demands a heart which is consecrated to him alone. His mercy understands that we go after selfish ambitions, and his grace wants to give us something so much better.

These afflictions can look like unjust suffering to us, but when we are given the grace of God to see them as he does, we can praise him for letting us stand in the remains of a life that would not have served as well. If God is taking our world apart, stripping us of our comforts and pulling away the false sources of hope and security, we can still recognize his mercy and give thanks.

God, give me your perspective so I can understand what you are doing in my life. And even when I don't understand it, help me trust you. If you are removing things from my life, I can only assume that they are not the best for your plan or for me.

LED BY FAITHFULNESS

In your faithfulness you have led the people whom you have redeemed; in your strength you have guided them to your holy habitation.

EXODUS 15:13 NASB

If you are a parent, you know the pain of watching your child experience disappointment. You wish you could protect them from the things that will hurt their hearts such as broken friendships, teasing, being left out, or missing out on exciting experiences. While it hurts to watch your child go through the slew of emotions that follow one of these issues, you also know that the things they encounter as children will help them for the rest of their lives, and therefore you support them through their pain but do not always rescue them from it.

God does the same with you as his child. Faithfully he leads you through the disappointments and hurts in life. He sees your pain, supports you and provides comfort, but he does not always pull you out of the trenches. He knows that what you face now will strengthen your character to be conformed to that of Christ's, and really, what could be better?

Lord, as I face disappointments or lead my family through them, help me remember that each one is not a surprise to you, but another tool that will help shape us into the image of Christ.

DELIGHTED

> "The LORD your God is with you;
> the mighty one will save you.
> He will rejoice over you.
> You will rest in his love;
> he will sing and be joyful about you."
>
> ZEPHANIAH 3:17 NCV

Many of us struggle to accept God's love. Sometimes in our frustration with ourselves and our struggle with the sin nature, we wish that God would punish us instead of extending mercy. Because of our pride it is easier to accept rejection than forgiveness; love is hard to receive when we deem ourselves unworthy of it.

But when we lay down our pride and let the grace of God's love flow into our hearts and cover our souls, we discover the joy of being found delightful. We should not allow anything to stop God's love from pouring into our lives today. We can take pleasure in knowing that he is looking for opportunities to love us despite our mistakes. Do not reject that love, dear friend. We can humble ourselves, open our hearts, and receive all the delight that he wants to pour over us.

God, it can be hard to know that despite my continued mistakes you constantly love me and want to show your delight in me. Help me to repent of my pride and my sin and receive all that you want to give me.

CONTENTMENT

My God will meet all your needs according
to the riches of his glory in Christ Jesus.

PHILIPPIANS 4:19 NIV

What do you have to have to be happy? Are you able to
delay or even forgo gratification? Contentment seems to
be a fading characteristic in our world, but the believer
must understand that Jesus went without things and was
willing to be content in all circumstances. Knowing that
Jesus was tempted, had unmet needs, and accepted what
was available to him can help us choose contentment for
our lives.

Pleasure is not something to seek at the expense of losing
our souls (Matthew 16:26), just as pain is not something
either that should be avoided at all costs. They are both
simply parts of life but just not the main focuses. We need
to assess whether or not we are demanding things from
God, from people, or from our circumstances. Do we think
we need these demands in order to be content? When we
remember Jesus and his circumstances, we should ask the
Spirit to give us the same grace that Jesus had, and then
be willing to accept what is available to us today.

Lord, forgive me for thinking that I need things to be a
certain way in order to be happy. You lived faithfully in less-
than-perfect circumstances, and by your grace I can too.

GLORIFY

The LORD is my strength and my shield;
in him my heart trusts, and I am helped;
my heart exults,
and with my song I give thanks to him.

PSALM 28:7 ESV

How are you glorifying the Lord today? Are you consciously aware of your charge to worship him—to see his power, majesty, goodness, and mercy, and to praise him for those amazing qualities? Or has the long to-do list already taken precedence in your mind today? It's a challenge to setting one's sights on God's goodness and glory instead of all that needs to be done on any given day, but we will never regret giving our energy to adoring God today.

Take a moment now to worship God. Has he shown himself faithful? Praise him for it. Have you witnessed his provision, a miracle, or his goodness? Glorify him. And if everything has gone wrong in your life, praise him still. If you can find no other reason to worship him aside from the fact that he has given you salvation, he is still worthy of *all* glory and honor!

God, in my busyness I forget to praise you. Help me be an active worshipper, one who sees your glory and goodness daily and never stops praising you for it.

Every Need Supplied

The young lions do without and suffer hunger;
but they who seek the LORD will not lack any good thing.
PSALM 34:10 NASB

It is easy to be tempted to lay up treasures on earth. With the increasing difficulty in finding what we need—like food—and the lack of stability in our world today, we want to give ourselves a safety-net in order to guard against trouble. A certain level of this is wise, allowing us to provide for our families in times of need. But we don't need to get so caught up in storing things that we begin to trust only ourselves and our stashes more than we trust the Lord.

Scripture promises that God's people will not go without: they will not be in want (Psalm 23:1); they lack no good thing (Psalm 31:10); God will supply every need according to his riches in Christ Jesus (Philippians 4:19). While it is important to be wise stewards of our resources, we need to seek first God's kingdom and his righteousness; his care of us will follow.

God, help me trust you more than I trust my own ability to provide for myself and my family. I want my life to be marked by striving to know you more, not striving to store up earthly treasures.

Unshakeable

The Lord's plans stand firm forever;
his intentions can never be shaken.
PSALM 33:11 NLT

How many times have the plans of man changed throughout history? It's impossible to know even the number of times our own plans change in one day, much less during the entirety of our lives. Essentially, things never go the way we think they will. That can be frustrating, or it can be enlightening. *Only* the plans of God stand firmly throughout time. They are impossible to shake or disrupt.

This should cause us to want to lay our plans at the feet of Christ on a daily, or sometimes hourly or moment-by-moment basis! We recognize that things do not usually unfold as we intend, and every time this happens, we have the privilege of acknowledging God's sovereignty over a situation. We thank God for knowing what is best for us and for releasing our expectations, so we learn to bow to his masterplan. What steps can we take today to let go of our uncertain plans and to trust the unshakeable plans of our Maker?

Lord, how good to know that while my life may never go as I intend, nothing can mess up your plans. Help me learn to be surrendered daily to your good and trustworthy plans for my life.

BEFRIENDING FAITHFULNESS

Trust in the Lord, and do good;
dwell in the land and befriend faithfulness.
Delight yourself in the Lord,
and he will give you the desires of your heart.
PSALM 37:3-4 ESV

The idea of being a friend to—befriending—faithfulness is probably not very exciting to many. Our culture thrives on new and exciting things. If we're bored with something, we move on, whether that is with TV shows, jobs, or relationships. Faithfulness, on the other hand, requires pushing through boredom, weariness, and difficulties. It means we don't give up when we don't like the situation anymore. It means that we do the thing that we were called to do without faltering because we value the end goal. We truly value the One who set the end goal and called us to the work in the first place.

Are you cultivating a friendship with faithfulness in your life? Are you trusting the Lord and believing that what he has called you to should be done with dedication and diligence even if you are weary or bored? Consider today how to befriend faithfulness in your life.

God, I am guilty of looking for the next new thing when I become tired of pressing through difficulties in my life. Help me see faithfulness to the task and to you as something to delight in, and not as a burden.

BLOOM

"God has made me fruitful in the land of my affliction."
GENESIS 41:52 NASB

Anyone who has ever had a garden understands that plants grow for a long time before they bear fruit. Seeds turn into sprouts, which grow into seedlings, then the plants mature. Only after several weeks of growth and good conditions will the plant begin to flower and bring forth fruit. If a short-sighted gardener thought of growth as only the bloom or only the vegetable, they would be sorely disappointed that it takes so long to achieve. They might even tear out the plant before it matured!

Just like plants, we grow throughout our lives and not just when we are blooming. All the trials we face are like the wind that causes the roots to grow down deeply into the soil to hold the plant firmly. We are preparing to bear fruit while we learn and mature. While the storms beat against us and while the sun shines down on us, we are growing in Christ. The measurement of our growth is not only in our blooms!

Thank you, Lord, that you are the one who causes me to grow and bear fruit. Help me see value in the journey, not just the finished product.

THE GOOD LIFE

What man is there who desires life
and loves many days, that he may see good?
Turn away from evil and do good;
seek peace and pursue it.
PSALM 34:12, 14 ESV

We all would likely admit that we want a good life. David knew this when he asked his rhetorical question in Psalm 34. Of course, man desires a good, long life full of happy days. Our efforts show this daily, and whether those efforts are self-pursuit or God-pursuit! But according to David there is a way to achieve this goal, and not many actually do it. He spoke in today's psalm about keeping the tongue from evil speech and lies, as well as turning away from wrongdoing and instead doing what is good.

Our lives show whether or not our priorities include elevating ourselves or slandering others. True happiness and peace come when we make the things God values most important: selflessness, kindness, speaking well of others, finding ways to honor others, and being peacemakers. What can we choose today to do the things that God says lead to a good life?

Lord, let me not spend my time making much of myself, but instead help me care for others, to speak with kindness, and to do what is right in your eyes.

INTERRUPTIBLE

When Jesus went out he saw a great multitude; and he was
moved with compassion for them, and healed their sick.
MATTHEW 14:14 NKJV

Jesus understood the need for solitude, and he regularly
took the opportunity to get away from the crowds and
even his closest friends in order to have time alone
with the Father. But he also understood the need for
compassion and the importance of taking hold of an
opportunity to be gracious to others.

We can all relate to the need for some personal space
and time alone. How often do we try to get away from
people for a little "me time"? We appreciate time away
from our spouse, friends, or children, but often we get
interrupted by a need. How should we respond to that
interrupted moment? Do we actually look at them the way
Jesus responded with his compassion? Or do we simply
feel irritated and frustrated when we have to deal with
someone else's problems? Today, we ask the Spirit to help
us be interruptible like Jesus was. May his gentleness and
graciousness be ours, too!

Lord, it can be so difficult to respond with compassion
when all I want is time by myself! Help me have a
compassionate heart as you did and help me be willing to
give of myself with love instead of annoyance.

GREEN PASTURES

He makes me lie down in green pastures.
He leads me beside still waters.
PSALM 23:2 ESV

The idea of Christ as our shepherd is not really one that most of us are unfamiliar with. Because of that we can sometimes miss the depth of meaning that accompanies this concept. Shepherds in biblical times were not grazing their sheep on the lush, grassy hills of the Irish countryside. Good pasture and clean water were scarce enough that the shepherd had to work hard to guide his sheep to green pastures so they would not go hungry or go without rest. Not only that, but the sheep would not lie down unless they felt safe, they were no longer hungry, and there weren't any pests amongst the flock. It took a lot of diligence on the shepherd's part to meet all these needs.

How much more does Christ our Shepherd go above and beyond to protect, guide, and supply for the needs of his sheep? Can we complain of any lack? Have we not been provided for in every way? We welcome the protective hand of our Good Shepherd who longs to lead us to green pastures.

Lord, may I learn to trust your hand which leads, guides, protects, comforts, and disciplines me. You have never led me astray and for that I am thankful.

CALL

Hear my prayer, LORD God Almighty;
listen to me, God of Jacob.
PSALM 84:8 NIV

The Lord loves to hear from us! Scripture tells us that his ears are attentive to our cries (Psalm 34:15). Compare this to a mother with her children; when a mom hears her child in distress, she doesn't ignore them and hope they will solve the problem on their own. No, she runs to them! In the same way, we have only to call upon the name of God and he will be right beside us to help, strengthen, and encourage us.

We may be facing temptations from people, Satan, or our own weaknesses, but we have victory when we call upon God and obey his guidance. He wants to hear our cries and respond to us, so we can share our struggles, our hurts, our hopes, and our dreams. He alone will help us stay the course which he has marked out for us.

Lord, how good you are to hear my cries for help. Help me to never think that I can accomplish things on my own; keep me humble and looking to you for help.

A BROKEN SPIRIT

The sacrifices of God are a broken spirit;
a broken and a contrite heart, God, you will not despise.
PSALM 51:17 NASB

God uses a lot of things in our lives to break us. The way we conduct our relationships, our responses to disagreeable authority, and circumstances when our pride and selfishness flare can all be opportunities for us to sacrifice in order to grow in Jesus. Why must we be broken? The answer is uncomfortable but necessary for growth: God loves a broken spirit, and that often comes in a person who is willing to embrace pain for his purposes.

Broken and contrite hearts can arise from the relational challenges in our lives such as our marriages, disagreeable children, bosses who do not honor others, or parents whom we can't understand. All these situations can cause our self-sufficiency to wear down until we have no choice but to come to God with our broken hearts, declaring our dependence upon him. He loves this, because he is then able to bind us up (Psalm 147:3), remove our guilt (Psalm 32:5), and purify us for his purposes (Titus 2:4).

Lord, I fight against pain and brokenness, but I see how you want in me a spirit that is willing to declare my need for you. Help me accept your methods for shaping my heart, even when it hurts so deeply.

GIVING UP GOOD

Blessed is the man who makes
the LORD his trust,
who does not turn to the proud,
to those who go astray after a lie!
PSALM 40:4 ESV

Sometimes we deceive ourselves. We think we are
pursuing the things of God because our passions are not
for obviously evil things. We don't spend copious amounts
of time with people who are living vile lives. We aren't
stealing, or lying, or cheating. We don't engage in behavior
that is obviously un-Christlike. But even good things can
distract us from chasing after the best things. God knows
our hearts better than we do, so we can ask him today
to reveal to us anything that we are pursuing which is
becoming too much of a distraction from what really
matters. It could be a relationship, or a hobby, or all those
good books on the bed stand. Even Martha was guilty of
cooking and cleaning when she was distracted from Christ
in the great story in Luke 10.

Ask the Spirit to show you the areas of your life that are
good, but not the best, and what he might want you to
surrender in order to have more of the very best thing.

God, forgive me for being distracted with good things to
the point of neglecting the best thing. Help me make you
my passion.

CULTIVATION

The fruit of righteousness is sown in peace
by those who cultivate peace.
JAMES 3:18 CSB

Cultivation takes time and effort. This is true for those
who cultivate land, such as plowing, planting, watering,
weeding, and harvesting. It is true for those who desire to
cultivate a skill or a characteristic. The qualities of Jesus that
we desire to be evident in our lives will not come naturally
to us; they must be nurtured. We must work at them,
dedicating intentional effort to becoming more like Jesus.

What aspect of the character of Christ do you desire to
emanate? Do you give your time and energy to cultivating
it? Or do you simply pray, "Lord, make me holy," and then
resist his efforts when he brings his sanctifying measures
into your life? Ask today what quality, what fruit he would
like you to cultivate in your life, and then work diligently
with the Spirit to grow in that direction.

God, I do want to grow in Christlikeness. I know it will
take effort on my part. Help me be willing to put in the
diligence necessary to see myself grow to be more like you.

I Remember You

My soul is downcast within me;
therefore I will remember you.
PSALM 42:6 NIV

Does deep sadness ever overtake you? Perhaps you have
sadness over a loss in your life, a struggle with sin, or over
some trial you face. Maybe there is pain that loved ones
are encountering and you feel it with them. Everyone has
probably suffered a downcast spirit at some point in our
lives. Pulling out of that despair can be one of the greatest
challenges.

The psalmist knew this struggle well, but he also knew
the antidote to the struggle: remembering God. The
tendency during a season of sorrow or depression can be
to shut God out. Someone stricken with depression can
internalize and see nothing but pain. But God is waiting,
and he will match pain with grace. Turning your gaze
heavenward in the midst of pain, choosing to worship God
in the midst of grief, will actually turn your mourning into
dancing, your sorrow into joy, and your pain into pleasure.
His grace is waiting for you.

Lord, it is easy to shut out everything when pain and sadness
take ahold of my heart. Help me not to be overcome by it,
but to make a conscious choice to worship you in the midst
of it. I know you will meet me with your grace.

REFINEMENT

Lift up your spears, both large and small,
against those who chase me.
Tell me, "I will save you."
PSALM 35:3 NCV

We love the idea of being saved from our troubles. A knight in shining armor swoops in to rescue us from all our ailments—it's such a sweet fairy tale that we wish we could live in real life. Sometimes we even take it so far as to wish the Lord would act as our knight, righting all that is wrong in our lives and rescuing us from our oppressors. We want to pray, as David did, that God would cast his spears and destroy those who wrong us.

But God is more interested in our refinement than our rescue. Sometimes his deliverance looks like he's leaving us in the battle to be sanctified rather than freeing us from that which causes us harm. Our desire to see an end come to our persecutors may seem justified, but it is likely motivated out of love for ourselves. God will pull us out of the fight when the refinement is complete for both sides of the battle. Trust the process.

Lord, I admit that I spend more time wishing for a rescue from oppression than I do asking how I can learn from the battle. Help me lean into you and see my sanctification as more important than my deliverance.

Unreasonable

Many are the woes of the wicked,
but the Lord's unfailing love
surrounds the one who trusts in him.
Psalm 32:10 niv

Things can seem unreasonably difficult sometimes. The kids get sick, we don't sleep, and the air conditioner goes out all on the same day. Our woes can feel so overwhelming and sometimes they are, but the difference between our trials and those of the unsaved is that we have a God who can be trusted to surround us with unfailing love in the midst of the reasonable and the unreasonable times.

What things are afflicting you today that you are finding unreasonable? How can you change your attitude toward your circumstances, remembering that every single thing you face is not faced alone? Set your sights on the unfailing love that surrounds you. Rest in it, be encouraged by it, and take ahold of it so you can face your woes with grace.

God, I know that in reality my trials are reasonable. You never promised an easy life for your followers. In fact, you let us know it would be hard! Forgive me for expecting and demanding ease with my complaining spirit. Help me accept the grace of your presence with me today.

UNDERSTANDING

Trust in the LORD with all your heart;
do not depend on your own understanding.
Seek his will in all you do,
and he will show you which path to take.

PROVERBS 3:5-6 NLT

Jane liked college for a particular reason that most people wouldn't have considered important: she had a clear course of action with very few decisions to make. As long as she stayed on the path laid out for her by the academic advisor, she would end up with a degree at the end of four years. It was great not to have to think about making plans and changing courses. But when college ended, she panicked. Now she was in charge of making all the decisions for the rest of her life. What if she messed up?

We often lean on our own understanding in life when we are making decisions. We do what makes sense to us, what is easy, or what we think will benefit us the most, naturally. But our understanding only goes so far, and when we come to an impasse, our best course of action is to surrender our plans, ideas, and expectations to the Lord. He will guide us if we allow him to speak into the path for our days and our lives.

Lord, help me not to get so caught up in how I understand life that I fail to seek your will when I am making decisions. I want to be led by you in all I do.

RESPONDING

By day the LORD directs his love,
at night his song is with me—
a prayer to the God of my life.
PSALM 42:8 NIV

Today's verse paints a picture of the Lord's relationship with us, the way he cares for us, and our responses to him. "By day, the Lord directs his love," speaks of his faithful love and mercy as our daily companion. His constant provision and protection remind us of his love. His acceptance of us despite our continual mistakes assures us of his gentle mercy.

And what is our response to him? "At night, his song is with me." Our thoughts at the end of the day should not be of all that went wrong or about the things we did not accomplish. Instead, we should be praising God for the way his love leads us through yet another day. In this way we will calm our anxieties by setting our minds on the goodness and grace of God. Does this psalm honestly reflect the way we interact with the Lord? The authors of this psalm present a compelling and beautiful interaction of God and his people.

God, I am often so caught up in the events of the day that I do not take time to notice your love woven throughout my moments. Help me be aware of your blessed mercy and to give the praise you are due in response.

CONVICTION

Search me, O God, and know my heart!
Try me and know my thoughts!
And see if there be any grievous way in me,
and lead me in the way everlasting!
PSALM 139:23-24 ESV

We know that the Word of God has the power to convict, reprove, and correct us. We are told in the words of today's psalm that the invitation for God to search us is poignant and valid. But when we read the Word and receive that conviction or instruction, is our tendency to receive it for someone else? Sin is blinding, and in particular we can be blind to the state of our own hearts. Unfortunately, this allows us to see the need for someone else to repent but fail to see our own need.

If this is your propensity when you read the Bible or listen to a sermon, ask the Holy Spirit to reveal to you your own sins instead of being concerned with the sins of others. God's Word exists to convict your heart, and it is your job to ensure that you alone are right before God. Pray as David did that God would search and know your heart, and then be prepared to deal with the sin which he reveals with a repentant spirit.

Lord, it is so easy to see where someone else has messed up, and to miss my own sin entirely. Please convict my heart so I can walk in righteousness before you.

BOASTING

In God we have boasted all day long,
and we will give thanks to your name forever.

PSALM 44:8 NASB

How often do we find ourselves boasting in the Lord—truly boasting in his strength, goodness, and mercy? As humans we latch onto anything that gives us a sense of self-confidence. That can lead us to dwell on our own strengths or we promote ourselves so that someone else recognizes in us as a gift or talent. Boasting then follows this inflated and poorly positioned confidence.

In God's mercy, however, we are allowed to see that our strengths are nothing without him. His mercy will even sometimes strip us of the things we boast about so we can clearly see the Lord's might and give him the glory he alone deserves. The next time we are tempted to pat ourselves on the back, we can instead take the opportunity to acknowledge God's power, goodness, and grace in our lives.

God, when things go well, I like to think that I am the one who has done all the good work. Really, though, you deserve all the glory. Without you I am nothing, and capable of nothing good on my own. Thank you for working through me, and may I only ever boast in you.

DELIGHTED

The Lord directs the steps of the godly.
He delights in every detail of their lives.
Though they stumble, they will never fall,
for the Lord holds them by the hand.
PSALM 37:23-24 NLT

As much as we fight against it, stumbling and struggling
are a part of life. We will never actually leave those
challenges behind until we reach eternity. We could allow
ourselves to be discouraged over this, or we can take joy
in Scripture's promise which assures us that our stumbling
will never do us in completely.

For those whose lives are committed to the way of
Christ, we know that God delights in every detail of our
lives. He sees our good days and our bad days. He finds
joy in the moments when we are conquering our fears,
serving tirelessly in our homes, leading someone to the
knowledge of the truth, or really struggling with pain and
self-doubt while seeking him. Like a mother who loves her
child regardless of whether they are accomplishing good
things or really messing up, God delights in us. He will
never allow our struggles to destroy us.

Jesus, thank you that you delight in me even when I am
really having a hard time. You know my struggles, you
are not upset with me, and you promise to be with me
through this. Thank you!

HE RESTORES

He restores my soul;
he guides me in the paths of righteousness
for the sake of his name.

PSALM 23:3 NASB

Do you ever feel like you are too far gone? You've made too many mistakes and surely you have disappointed God too many times for him to waste any more of his time on you, right? Satan would have us believe that as a truth. He wants us to think that God can't restore us, or even if he could, he wouldn't want to. Nothing can be further from the truth, though! God offers wholeness to even the parts of us which we would consider a lost cause.

Are there parts of you that you don't believe can be restored and made whole again? Confess your unbelief and pray for the faith to believe in his restoring power. There is nothing he cannot do, and he wants to bring restoration to you not only for your own sake, but for the sake of his glory, too!

God, forgive me for my lack of belief in your power to bring healing and make my broken places whole again. You do not see me as a lost cause, and you are not tired of working with me. Restore my soul, Savior.

No Impasse

It was not by their sword that they won the land,
nor did their arm bring them victory;
it was your right hand, your arm,
and the light of your face, for you loved them.

PSALM 44:3 NIV

One thing made very clear in the Old Testament is that it was not by Israel's own strength and might that they defeated their foes, survived in the wilderness, or took possession of the Promised Land. It was by God's hand alone that these things happened; he took care of the obstacles that lay in their path. He dealt with the things that looked like a total impasse to human understanding. Ultimately, it was God's favor on the Israelites that led them past these roadblocks.

God will do the same for you, too. Are you facing what looks like a dead end today? Surrender your obstacle to the Lord and he will uproot and displace what he needs to happen in order to plant you where you need to be. Do not attempt to do it by your own power. We know from Israel's history that these things are best left to the Lord.

God, thank you for reminding me that it is your power alone that allows me to flourish. Help me turn to you when I am facing a dead end, knowing that you are capable of bringing me to the best possible place.

EVER-PRESENT HELPER

God is our protection and our strength.
He always helps in times of trouble.
PSALM 46:1 NCV

Do you have any fair-weather friends? These friends stick close by as long as things are going well in your life, but as soon as times turn tough and you could use some help, they disappear. There is nothing more frustrating than realizing that the people you thought cared about you had no good intentions for the friendship after all.

What comfort we find then in knowing that God is not this kind of friend. If every little thing is going wrong in our lives or in the world, he will still be found with us. He's not hoping to get something out of the relationship; he's simply present as a father and a true friend. He is always with us in times of trouble; not just when it's convenient for him, not just when he didn't already have other plans, and not just because there was no one else who could assist. We can reach out to our ever-present helper first. His help is a guaranteed, "Yes!"

God, thank you that I can count on you to be with me as my helper, and not fear that I will be left on my own to figure the hard stuff out. I am so thankful for your faithfulness toward me.

REDEEMED BY GRACE

God will redeem my life.
he will snatch me from the power of the grave.
PSALM 49:15 NLT

This world trusts in their riches. The materialistic mindset of recent generations pervades every aspect of life now, tempting us to believe that unless we have the newest and the best, and more and more of it, our lives are lacking. But Scripture reminds us that all of the good things the world offers will pass away. In this age of social media comparison, it is easy to feel like someone else's life is better than our own, but in the end, is it really?

If you are living with the goal of eternal riches in mind, then all the good things your friends and neighbors have should not faze you. Do not get caught up in all that you supposedly lack and put your hope in what will actually last and redeem you when all is said and done.

Oh Lord, give me eyes to see the benefits of storing up eternal riches. Let me not get caught up in the comparison game or buy into the idea that I am lacking anything. I have you and there is nothing I lack!

TODAY

Use every chance you have for doing good,
because these are evil times.
EPHESIANS 5:16 NCV

Twenty-four hours really isn't much time. Take out the time we spend sleeping, and we're left with maybe sixteen hours each day for productivity, enjoyment, and building our relationships with the Lord. But how many hours out of our days do we spend being overly concerned about the future, or analyzing days gone by? If we could see the minutes that add up to hours over our lifetimes that have been spent in anxious thoughts and worry, we would probably be ashamed.

Today is a gift. There has never been another like it. And no matter how your days feel—joyful or monotonous, adventurous or relaxed, simple or challenging—you will never get this time back once it is gone. Rejoice in it, therefore! Ask God how he would have you use the limited hours to best glorify him and enjoy the gift of today.

Lord, I do not want to waste the time you have given me by worrying about things in my past or the future. Help me take hold of today with enthusiasm and give you my best.

GRACE DAY

The LORD delights in his people;
he crowns the humble with victory.
PSALM 149:4 NLT

God delights in his people, and sometimes that delight manifests in a grace day. Grace days are those when you know the joy of the Lord deep down in your soul, even when the odds are stacked against you; despite the challenges nothing can steal your joy. A grace day can look like this: you respond with compassion to your whiny children and feel only love, not annoyance, toward them. They are the days when the sin nature seems to have lost all its power over you and you feel overtaken by the Spirit, bearing good fruit.

Give thanks to your gracious God on these days, but do not despair when not all days are this way. It is God's pleasure in us that allows us to have these special days. They are a sweet taste of what is coming in eternity. Praise the Lord there will be days in heaven when every day is a grace day!

Lord, while I wish that every day could be so full of your joy, grace, and love, I am thankful for the days when your presence is so obvious to me. Thank you for delighting in me. May I persevere through the difficult days, knowing that in eternity all struggles will be no more.

JULY

How sweet your
word is to my taste—
sweeter than honey
in my mouth.

PSALM 119:103 CSB

SUMMON

The Mighty One, God the LORD,
speaks and summons the earth
from the rising of the sun to its setting.
PSALM 50:1 ESV

Do you ever stop to think about how God causes all things to happen? He didn't create the world and set it in motion, watching from a distance as it runs its course. He summons the earth daily, causing the sun to rise and set, seeds to sprout, and hearts to be softened to his calling.

He is daily, intimately, involved in your life, too. His magnificent power is personal. He knows your life and is closely involved in all your activities. He summons you to awaken each morning, work with diligence within your calling, and sense his presence and love in your life. "What is man that you are mindful of him?" (Psalm 8:4). And yet he is! Be encouraged by his mindfulness of you today, and by the way he acts with you.

Thank you, Lord, that you are not just some distant being watching the world. You are involved in my life, and in the lives of every person and created thing. May I be ever more aware of your participation in my life, and may I never attempt to live my life without your direction.

Pruning

The LORD disciplines those he loves,
and he punishes everyone he accepts as his child.
HEBREWS 12:6 NCV

Experienced gardeners know the benefits of pruning their plants. To the untrained eye pruning looks painful to the plant, causing it to look bare, or even like it will die! But the gardener knows that pruning is for the plant's good; he is taking away anything that will not allow it to flourish.

God acts the same way in the lives of his children. He prunes and disciplines, pulling away from us anything that will not be for our good. It may be painful at the time, and it might even feel like we're dying, but his processes are meant to help us grow. Don't be resistant to the gardener's shears, painful as it may be. Let him cut away the things that will not help growth. It is his deep love for us that causes him to act in this way.

God, help me to not resist your discipline. I know it is because you are full of love and mercy for me that you remove the things which will not help me. May my heart be soft and open to your pruning.

LIKED AT OUR WORST

I will be glad and rejoice in your mercy,
for you have considered my trouble;
you have known my soul in adversities.
PSALM 31:7 NKJV

We tend to like ourselves best when we are strong, productive, and capable. When we prove to ourselves and to the world just how much we can accomplish, then we feel satisfied. The world tells us this is what we must aim for by doing our best at all times.

As we know by now, God is pretty countercultural. He prefers the opposite of what the world and our natural selves would call good. What does that mean in this context? It means that God likes us best when we are weak. He takes pleasure in our weak glances toward him, admitting our need. He loves it when we come to the end of ourselves and rest our eyes on him, because it is then that he can clothe us in mercy and strength. Do not despise weaknesses, friend.

God, it is hard to feel like I'm "not all that." I don't like me when I'm weak, so it is hard to understand how you do! But help me to rejoice in my weaknesses and see them as opportunities to be clothed in your strength.

CHOOSE THEREFORE

You are my strength, I sing praise to you;
you, God, are my fortress,
my God on whom I can rely.
PSALM 59:17 NIV

Even if you are a morning person, mornings aren't always easy. Kids make demands and rush to get out the door on time. You have to deal with unforeseen challenges after not getting enough rest or coffee. It can cause selfishness to rise. It takes a conscious choice to joyfully proclaim God's love and faithfulness in these moments. God is your stronghold. He provides all the strength and grace you need for the day ahead whether you are well rested or not, whether you have to deal with crabby children or angels, and whether you dread your workday or you're enthusiastic about it.

Choose, therefore, to sing praise to God, your fortress. Choose, therefore, to put your hope in the saving grace of Christ and not in your circumstances. Choose, therefore, to bless the Lord each morning whether you slept well or not. You can rely on him.

Lord, I am glad that you do not leave me on my own to face each new day. Your mercies are new for me today and I have all I need to walk in godliness, even when things are less than perfect. Help me choose to worship and declare your goodness and faithfulness today.

LIGHT AND TRUTH

There I will go to the altar of God,
to God—the source of all my joy.
I will praise you with my harp,
O God, my God!
PSALM 43:4 NLT

We will be fighting battles our whole lives. We will have to ward off sin, worldly and demonic temptations, and oppression by those who believe we are foolish. When we are in the thick of the battle, we can pray for God's light and truth to lead us. There is never a more important time to know the truth than when we are being crushed, oppressed, or deceived. We can reach out for the truth that Scripture offers; we are persecuted but not abandoned; struck down but not destroyed (2 Corinthians 4:9). We have victory over sin and death through the Lord Jesus Christ (1 Corinthians 15:57). We do not belong to those who shrink back and are destroyed, but to those who have faith and are saved (Hebrews 10:39).

We can make a conscious choice to put our hope in the truth when everything around us tries to keep us from praising God. We have the victory!

God, thank you for your Word that speaks truth into every situation I face. Help me to be aware of when I need your light and truth to lead me. May I not try to fight the battle on my own.

LIKE JESUS

We are God's children now, and what we will be has not
yet appeared; but we know that when he appears we shall
be like him, because we shall see him as he is.

1 JOHN 3:2 ESV

This promise from 1 John brings comfort on days when we
are struggling to feel like we will ever be fully sanctified.
The "will be but not yet" promise which believers live with
keeps us thankful for the gift of holiness over us now but is
also keeps us longing for the day when full sanctification
will happen. Just imagine when we will be like Jesus:
humble, kind, gracious, and full of mercy. These are all the
things we long to be but are not yet.

We could let discouragement overrule our hearts when
our struggle to be like Christ continues day after day.
Alternatively, we could hope in the promise that one day
all our struggles will pass away, and we will be like Jesus.
We set our sights on that promise today, and we keep on
keeping on.

Jesus, when I become frustrated over my struggles with
sin, help me hope in the promise that when I see you, I
will be made like you. There will be no more struggles, no
more sin, and no more temptation. How I long for that
day. Fill me with your power to live well today.

Faithful

"I will betroth you to me in faithfulness.
Then you will know the Lord."
HOSEA 2:20 NASB

The human understanding of faithfulness is skewed due to our experiences. Imperfect displays of faithfulness are all around us. We pledge love but easily dismiss it when it no longer works. If our needs are not being met at church, we leave to find another one. True faithfulness means a commitment through painful experiences, difficult communication, and unmet expectations. When our commitment, based solely on our human understanding, waivers, we wonder how we can be faithful to such hard tasks.

When we read about Christ as our faithful bridegroom, we wonder how he can love us in spite of our wandering hearts. But his faithfulness is all him; it has nothing to do with our ability to stay true to him. He has made a covenant and he will not break his promise. Thank him today for his faithfulness that is not reliant on you but upon him alone.

Lord, it is comforting to know that when you are faithful to your promise, it is not dependent upon my perfection. Help me understand your love which sees beyond my mistakes so I can walk in that same kind of faithfulness.

OUR LEADER FOREVER

He is our God forever and ever,
and he will guide us until we die.
PSALM 48:14 NLT

Psalm 48 is a joyous declaration of God's power displayed in Zion. It ends with a challenge to the reader to tell future generations about the God who leads his people forever. How are you living today in such a way that this message will be passed on to future generations? Does your life reflect the belief that your God will always lead you and those you love? Do you live your days in peace as you trust God's leading, or do you have an anxious heart?

Take a serious look at your life today and ask yourself if the way you are living reflects a deep trust in God's leadership. Has he done something you don't understand? What was your response? Ask yourself how you can display a peaceful trust in God's plan to your children, friends, and family. Declare your joy in God as he leads you with faithfulness your whole life.

Lord, I am guilty of responding in frustration or anger when something happens that I don't understand. Forgive my unbelief! You have always led me faithfully and will continue to do so. May my life reflect complete trust in you.

NOT IN VAIN

Be steadfast, immovable, always abounding in the work of the LORD, knowing that in the LORD your labor is not in vain.
1 CORINTHIANS 15:58 ESV

Jesus didn't face easy circumstances during his earthly life. His teachings caused more people to dislike him than to follow him; the people he came to save rejected him; his miracles and motives were questioned repeatedly. What if he had just called it quits when he wasn't seeing fruit from his labor?

We will often work hard at something without seeing the fruit we hope for, but Jesus calls us to faithful living even when the fruit doesn't necessarily match the effort. Jesus pushed through to victory, and he offers us that same victory over our weariness. What are we pushing hard for today without seeing the results we are hoping for? We can ask the Holy Spirit to refresh our souls and give us the grace to be steadfast in our work.

Jesus, thank you for not giving up in your ministry even when things weren't looking positive. Help me to also stand strong in the work you have called me to, whether I see the fruit of my labor or not. I know that everything I do for you will not be for nothing!

TRUE LIFE

"I am the resurrection and the life. Whoever believes in me,
though he die, yet shall he live, and everyone who lives
and believes in me shall never die. Do you believe this?"

JOHN 11:25-26 ESV

How do you define *living*? Does it resemble the definition
the rest of the world gives? Do you aspire to good
experiences, success in career and family, or legacies to
pass on to the next generation? Or are you okay with
living that is more defined by dying? Are you comfortable
making sacrifices in order to bring the good news to
someone just so you can glorify God, and thereby deny
your own opportunities to boast in yourself? Does *living*
for you mean serving faithfully without necessarily ever
hearing any thanks?

Take a close look and ask yourself what kind of life you
have now. Is it a type that looks like everyone else, or does
your life look like the one Jesus offered. Do not be afraid
to embrace a life of sacrifice. There is untold beauty in
denying yourself so Jesus may be glorified!

Lord, I admit that my life often looks like that of the rest
of the world. Help me to be okay with not having the
success other people have, or not being recognized for my
hard work. I know that any sacrifice I make for you will be
rewarded far beyond what my earthly reward could be.
The life you offer appeals so much more to me!

ENOUGH FOR TODAY

The LORD is my shepherd,
I will not be in need.
PSALM 23:1 NASB

Sometimes the Lord gives bountifully, and sometimes he gives incrementally, but he will meet our needs. Scripture tells us that his mercies are new for us every morning, but it doesn't say that we can collect mercy from one day and apply it to the next. Like the Israelites in the wilderness who were provided the manna they needed for a day at time, so too God provides for us each day; but sometimes it's specifically for a day at a time.

Accept what he has given you for this day and praise him for it is enough. Rest in the goodness of his provision and do not worry about tomorrow. Repeat this to yourself as often as you need to today: the Lord is my shepherd; I will not be in need.

God, I often find myself worrying and anxious when you have already given me grace and mercy that is sufficient for today. Help me to not worry about tomorrow, knowing that there are new mercies awaiting me for all that I will face later.

TENDERNESS

The LORD is merciful and gracious,
slow to anger, and abounding in mercy.
PSALM 103:8 NKJV

If you are a parent, you've probably been harsh with your kids at times, maybe more often than you would like to admit. As a child, you probably experienced harsh words or attitudes from your parents as well. How interesting to think, then, that God does not relate to us as an upset parent does. He doesn't yell, scold, or belittle us when we are struggling. He is slow to anger, gentle, tender, and full of compassion.

You, my friend, move the heart of God even on the days you are grouchy and annoyed. His compassion pulls you toward him; he is not put off by your scrapes and fleshly desires. All of him loves you, and all of him wants good for you. How is he showing his tenderness to you today? How can you reflect that tenderness toward others?

God, it humbles me when I think about the compassion that abounds from your heart in the midst of my struggles. How good you are to respond in kindness instead of anger when I can't seem to get it together. May that mercy change my heart and cause me to respond in gentleness toward others also.

BURDEN BEARER

Praise be to the LORD, to God our Savior,
who daily bears our burdens.
PSALM 68:19 NIV

You know those secret things you carry in your heart—the quiet burdens that you don't tell anyone about for fear that they won't understand or that you will be judged or rejected? You need to know something about them: you don't actually carry those burdens alone. Psalm 68 tells us that day after day the God of our salvation bears our burdens. How good to know that what we think we are carrying alone, he takes off our shoulders because he sees and cares.

What are you carrying in your heart today that you can release to the Lord? Remember that his yoke is easy, and his burden is light (Matthew 11:30). He will gladly trade your burden for his light and easy load. Accept it for yourself today.

Lord, how comforting it is to know that the things that weigh me down do not need to be carried alone, and they aren't! You carry these burdens for me daily, even when I am unaware of it. Thank you so much for the way you care for me.

STUCK

"Fear not, for I am with you;
be not dismayed, for I am your God;
I will strengthen you, I will help you,
I will uphold you with my righteous right hand."

ISAIAH 41:10 ESV

Have you ever watched a stream tumble down waterfalls and around rocks? Perhaps as a child you threw leaves or pinecones into the water, watching and hoping they would make it downstream. Inevitably some of them would get caught in the eddies, swirling and swirling around the rocks but unable to journey on without a helping hand.

Sometimes life can feel like that swirling leaf. You get caught in a life-size eddy, unable to free yourself from bad habits and struggles with sin. When you find yourself in that place do not be dismayed, for it is not you who must pull yourself out of the spiral. The righteous right hand of God will help you. He has the power to free you from the confines of your flesh. He will not leave you to save yourself. Look to him for the assistance you need to continue your journey.

God, it feels sometimes that I will struggle with certain things forever. Thank you for not leaving me to pull myself out of the eddy; you will help me. May I never take my eyes off of the one who saves me.

ALL TIMES

Trust in him at all times, you people;
pour out your hearts before him;
God is a refuge for us.
PSALM 62:8 NASB

We are commanded a lot in the Bible to trust God, but today's verse really makes *when* to trust him eminently clear: "Trust in him at all times, you people." When his blessings are bountiful, trust him. When everything falls apart, trust him. When life is steady, trust him. When everything is not stable, trust him. When your heart is at peace, trust him. When you are in turmoil, trust him. At all times, trust him.

Let him hear your cries, your moans, your praise, and your joy. Let him hear it all because there is nothing that will surprise him. Nothing will send him reeling; nothing that will cause him to turn his back on you. And at the end of it all, declare your trust in him and watch him carry you through.

Thank you, Lord, that you are a refuge for me. Thank you that I can share with you the things that shake me up and knock me down and at the end of it all you are still just waiting for me to say, "I trust you." You are so good!

MEEK

"Blessed are the meek,
for they shall inherit the earth."
MATTHEW 5:5 NKJV

Meekness is a characteristic that most people would not list on their resume. To us it has connotations of weakness. A meek person seems to be a push-over, unable to stand their ground. Jesus' countercultural statement in this Beatitudes verse today rubs against our natural instinct to fight for our rights, reject criticism, and go for the win.

Yet when we are meek, we understand God's grace more. When we set aside our need to be right or to defend ourselves and prove our worth, we understand how wretched we really are and how our souls are in desperate need of mercy. When we embrace the humility of Christ, our eyes are opened to the blessedness of accepting our weaknesses and seeing Christ's glorious grace.

God, help me see the areas of my life where I need to embrace meekness so I can recognize my need for your grace. May I never be too proud to miss opportunities for your mercy.

GUIDANCE

"I will make you wise and show you where to go.
I will guide you and watch over you."
PSALM 32:8 NCV

Fear of the unknown can feel like the enemy sometimes.
It keeps us trapped in worry and anxiety about what
might happen, or what we might miss out on, or what
might go wrong if we go in the wrong direction. In reality,
the enemy is self-reliance; it is harmful to believers to
think that we can make all the best choices for ourselves
without the need for God's guidance.

We don't need to have all of our steps lined up perfectly
in order to make progress; we need only to rely on God to
give us what we need to know when we need to know it.
What have you been trusting yourself with lately? What
unknowns have you been fearing instead of trusting the
Lord's good guidance? Give to him each day, each step,
each situation that scares you and each opportunity to
either trust yourself or trust the Lord. Let him be your
guide today.

Jesus, my tendency to trust myself or to give in to fear
usurps my trust in your good directions. Forgive me for my
lack of faith and help me to live a life surrendered to you.

DROUGHT

You crown the year with a bountiful harvest;
even the hard pathways overflow with abundance.
PSALM 65:11 NLT

Another year of drought. That lush green season that you longed for all winter simply never came. Is God still near in those seasons of drought? Is his care still present when the bountiful harvest has no chance of happening? Sometimes drought comes to our souls as well as our crops. Challenges in relationships drain us, joy is hard to come by. Where is God then?

Whether we feel it or not, God's care for us has not ended even when dry seasons linger. His goodness continues to crown our lives, and eventually we will see signs of growth again. Our mandate is to sing even when the grass doesn't grow, and the streams dry up. Sing, even when the pain doesn't leave, and trouble continues. We praise him because he is worthy of praise, not because all is right in our world.

Lord, sometimes these challenging seasons seem to go on and on. Help me remember that they, too, will come to an end. In the meantime, may I continue to praise you even when all has gone wrong.

MAJESTY

LORD my God, you are very great;
you are clothed with splendor and majesty.
PSALM 104:1 NIV

How do you experience the majesty of God? Is it in the colors of the sunset? Does your heart tug at you with the smiles and coos of a new baby? God's majesty may seem like something that is found only in big events or experiences, but really it is to be found in everything from the magnificent to the monotonous.

When was the last time you encountered God's splendor and majesty? If it feels like it has been a long time since you were "wowed" by God, ask him to reveal more of it to you again. But don't forget to look for it in the mundane moments of ordinary life, either. Look up, expect it, and search for it. See what incredible things God shows you when you ask him for more revelations of his glory. Prepare to be amazed.

God, I get so caught up in normal life that I forget to look for your beauty and majesty in the small, ordinary things. Help me recognize your glory in the big and the small, and to give you the praise due to you.

FAMILIAR WEAKNESS

I love you, O LORD, my strength.
The LORD is my rock and my fortress and my deliverer,
my God, my rock, in whom I take refuge,
my shield, and the horn of my salvation, my stronghold.
PSALM 18:1-2 ESV

Sometimes we recognize God's power and strength in the big things in life which familiarize us again with our need for dependence on him. But what about the mundane weaknesses that we face repeatedly, even daily? Should we scorn the things that plague us? Or should we see them as opportunities to praise him and find him to be strong in those routine flaws?

We do not need to resent our weaknesses. We can use those small but trying things as reminders of his power over all troubles in this world (John 16:33). Hard as it might be, we can even thank him for our pain, sorrow, and discomfort. By doing so we are saved from the enemy; the weaknesses that used to send us into despair are now sending us back to the throne of the King.

Lord, you didn't come to save me just from major events, but from the trials that I will face repeatedly. Help me surrender my weaknesses to you.

GROWING SLOWLY

The LORD is good to those who await him,
to the person who seeks him.
LAMENTATIONS 3:25 NASB

Our world today tends to rush everything: fast food, instant grocery delivery, and kids reading by four years of age. If we take our time in something, peer pressure makes us feel like we are doing it wrong. In reality, slow growth is okay. In the Christian life, there isn't a fast-track to holiness or bearing good fruit, but even there we can feel like we should be further along than we are.

God takes delight in slow growth for his children. We are a blessing to God when we are satisfied to grow at his pace. Often that means plenty of delays that we would rather avoid or feeling like we take two steps forward and one step back. There is comfort in this truth, however: the Lord is good to those who wait for him, even if that means persisting longer than we had hoped for our change from sinful to sanctified. It's okay with growing slowly. We will still bloom in the end.

Lord, I get frustrated with myself when I feel like I should be further along in my walk than it seems like I am. In those moments, help me wait upon and seek you. You know how long this journey will take; I can trust you.

Love from a Friend

"You, Israel, are my servant,
Jacob whom I have chosen,
the descendants of Abraham my friend."

Isaiah 41:8 NKJV

Since the days of Abraham, God's people have been known as his friends. We don't simply belong to him like a cat belongs to its owner; we are actually his friends! His care of us, therefore, isn't just to keep us alive but to make his love known to us. Sometimes friends will do nice things to show their love on days when we need a pick-me-up.

God does the same with his children. He uses little things to remind us of his love and to let us know that we are seen and remembered. We can think of these quiet considerations as "love notes from God" which he leaves for us to find, just like a friend would leave a note on our car windshield to be discovered after work. What kinds of things remind us of God's love? If we pay attention, we will soon see how often God sends his love to his beloved daughter "just because."

God, thank you that you look for ways to show me your love. May I never be too busy or too caught up in my own concerns to not notice the little ways you display your love for me.

GOD OF THE VALLEYS

God, my strength, I am looking to you,
because God is my defender.
PSALM 59:9 NCV

It often seems that God often leads his people into life events that are too big, too unfamiliar, too intimidating, and too overwhelming for us to handle on our own. Life isn't mostly straight paths lined with rainbows. It's steep and rocky with trails that wind into dark valleys where everything feels more difficult than we are expecting.

Whether we are walking under rainbows or running through rainstorms, if we look to God for our strength, we will find that he is faithful for everything we need with each new challenge ahead. Every scary circumstance is another opportunity to declare God to be our defender and to admit our need for him. If we are uncertain as to how we should parent our growing child, God has us covered. If we are facing choices that we never expected to face, the Lord will direct us. We keep our eyes on him and he will not let us go through the valley alone.

God, sometimes I get overwhelmed by each new challenge. Sometimes it seems that they never let up. Help me look to you and know that you will give me all I need to keep pressing on.

Rejoicing in His Shadow

Because you are my help,
I sing in the shadow of your wings.
PSALM 63:7 NIV

In the middle of summer, we rejoice in the blessings which bring relief from the heat such as a cold drink, a swim in the lake, or a refreshing breeze in the shade of a mature tree. Likewise, we also rejoice in whatever brings relief from the stresses and perils of life; for those who love God, it is rest in the shadow of his wings.

If life has been anxious lately, take some time to step away from what you can and find rest and relief in the comforting protection of your Helper. Take your attention off the things that are hard or not going well and direct your focus to God, giving him praise that he is good even when things around you are not. Rejoice and find peace as you rest under his protective wings.

Thank you, God, that you offer a place of refreshment when I am weary from the difficult things in my life. I take joy in knowing that I can always step into the shadow of your wings to find rest and peace for my soul.

POWER STRUGGLES

"For the LORD will vindicate his people
and have compassion on his servants,
when he sees that their power is gone."
DEUTERONOMY 32:36 ESV

Power struggles with little kids are no joke. A toddler will wear herself out demanding that she is right and fighting for what she wants. She will insist with her last breath that her parent has no idea what they're talking about. But after the toddler finally loses her strength, the sweetest thing occurs. Instead of the parent getting in the child's face with reprimands or victory dances, their compassion consumes them. They lovingly embrace the child and gently set them on the right path. There is no haughtiness in their manner; only love for their child.

This is how God sees us. We might kick and scream against God's way, insisting that we know what is best for us. But when we finally admit our responsibility in the matter, God's response is only compassionate and joyful that we have come back to him.

Lord, thank you for responding with such mercy when I have stubbornly maintained that I am right. Forgive me and help me see my need for your loving guidance.

HE LIKES YOU

The LORD takes pleasure in all he has made!
PSALM 104:31 NLT

We all have things that we don't like about ourselves like the way we laugh, our defensiveness when we're criticized, or a weak aspect of our character. These things make us self-conscious and keep us awake at night as we overthink and wonder how others perceive us.

When it comes to God, we might be tempted to think that he simply tolerates us, especially the parts of ourselves that we consider less than wonderful. But he doesn't just tolerate us; he likes us. Psalms says he takes pleasure in all he has made, which includes the things that we might find detestable. We can be bold and bring before him the parts of ourselves that we don't like. We don't need to fix or change anything initially, but just to have him receive us and love us. He will not reject us, scorn us, or laugh at us; he will find each of us altogether lovely (Song of Solomon 4:7).

God, I have a hard time accepting all the imperfect parts of me, but I am thankful that you see me as lovely. Thank you that I can come before you with boldness, knowing that there is no part of me you simply tolerate—you love it all!

No Enemy Too Great

He will send from heaven and save me;
he will put to shame him who tramples on me.
God will send out his steadfast love and his faithfulness!
PSALM 57:3 ESV

When he wrote this psalm, David's enemies were legitimately trying to take his life, but your enemies and mine are likely to be more subtle and not so life-threatening. Even so, enemies do pursue us in all different seasons and for different reasons. Maybe for you it is an oppressive authority figure or circumstances out of your control. Perhaps your current enemy is the fear within you.

Life-threatening or not, God serves as our protector, and he will vindicate us in the face of our enemies. It is not solely our responsibility to fight off all that menaces or oppressors us; God will fight on our behalf. We can ask today that he would serve as our protector in the face of our enemies. We can release to him our struggles and pray for his steadfast love and faithfulness to cover us.

Lord, I know that you are in control, but sometimes I struggle to believe that you will protect me in the face of my enemies. I choose today to release to you my enemies and ask that you will fight on my behalf. I know that on my own I cannot adequately protect myself.

BETTER PLANS

Do not put your trust in princes,
in human beings, who cannot save.
When their spirit departs, they return to the ground;
on that very day their plans come to nothing.
PSALM 146:3-4 NIV

Maria was so excited to have her parents visit. It was
months since they were together, and she longed for
the good connection and new memories between her
children and their grandparents. Within a couple days of
their arrival, however, they all got sick. Instead of taking
adventures, they hid away in their respective rooms,
miserable and missing each other. Maria was disappointed
and angry with God. Didn't he know how much she
needed this time with her parents?

Life has a way of disappointing us, and if we are set on our
plans actually happening, we will end up bitter with God
and anyone else who can be blamed. If we set our minds
instead on the goodness of God's plan which cannot be
thwarted, that gives us a new perspective which will help
us overcome any disappointment.

God, I do tend to put too much hope in plans happening
as I have envisioned them. Help me put my hope in you
instead of the fulfillment of my desires.

MERCY TO KEEP YOU

"The Father gives me the people who are mine. Every one of them will come to me, and I will always accept them."
JOHN 6:37 NCV

Imagine this: you messed up big time and need to confess to your friend. You know it's likely they'll end up pushing you away, but your conscience won't let you off the hook. You summon all your courage, approach them, and sincerely apologize. They are disappointed in your behavior, but to your complete amazement, they forgive you fully, thanking you for your honesty.

It seems to us sometimes that our mistakes are simply too big to bring to Jesus. Surely, he will no longer count us among his people. But when we bring our mistakes to him, we find, instead of rejection, complete forgiveness, and absolute mercy. There is no mistake too great, no doubt too big, no lack of faith too extreme that can remove you from his family. Are you feeling down on yourself? Consider his incredible mercy that receives you and keeps you.

Lord, I am so unworthy of your love that keeps me despite my many, terrible mistakes. Help me receive your mercy and always be willing to confess to you. Thank you for accepting all of me.

WITH YOU

"I will certainly be with you."
EXODUS 3:12 NKJV

Perhaps you need to be reminded of this simple but powerful promise today. We don't know what anyone else is facing, but the Lord does, and he will certainly be with you in it. Taking on a new role in your job? He will certainly be with you. Approaching a friend to confront a sin? He will certainly be with you. Attempting to restore a relationship with an estranged child? He will certainly be with you.

This promise was spoken to Moses, but it is true for us as well. No matter what you face in your days, he will certainly be with you. God gives grace, boldness, wisdom, power, and compassion. He knows what you need, and he is with you to supply it.

God, it is easy to forget that there is nothing in my life that I face alone. Help me know your presence in the big and scary things as well as the small and mundane. I do not go alone, so let me never believe the lie that I face my days without your grace and power.

A TASTE OF HOME

"No one has ever seen this,
and no one has ever heard about it.
No one has ever imagined
what God has prepared for those who love him."
1 CORINTHIANS 2:9 NCV

You are an alien and stranger on earth. Do you ever
contend with that idea? It's probable that part of you
wants to belong. You might want to belong to a certain
lifestyle, a home, or to someone special, and yet you
belong only to Christ. He is your only claim in this life. But
God, in his grace, has given you tastes of belonging. This
is not to tease you but to encourage you to keep holding
out for the best that is coming in eternity.

What tastes of belonging have you experienced lately? Is
there joyous laughter in your home, deep rest at night, or
sweet fellowship in church? Do you see that these precious
times allow you to revel in the beauty and majesty of
creation? Recognize these gifts, but do not rest in a
shadowy vision of what is to come; do not make this your
home. Don't become content with counterfeit happiness.

God, in the moments when I long to belong, help me
remember that I have only glimpses of the glory that awaits
me in heaven.

AUGUST

Taste and see
that the LORD is good.
Oh, the joys of those
who take refuge in him!

PSALM 34:8 NLT

NOT OUR OWN

I know, LORD, that our lives are not our own.
We are not able to plan our own course.
JEREMIAH 10:23 NLT

How long will it take us to understand that our lives are the Lord's, not the Lord's *and* ours? Perhaps we are still learning this. Many of us still don't understand that life is a gift. However, we often try to take ownership of it when we were never really meant to. "*My* life is busy," we say. "All of these things are messing up *my* plans."

At some point we must choose to surrender our lives to Jesus. Without this we will continue to feel like we are fighting against him as our plans for our lives don't go as we expect. It takes awareness and strength from the Lord to open our hands and tell him today that we need to surrender. Do we still insist that we plan some aspect of life? If we pray for the grace to release it to the Lord, we will find it the perfect path designed by God for each of us.

Lord, I do not want to live my life fighting to hold on to my own way. I know I will only become bitter when things don't go the way I want. Help me to surrender to you every aspect of life, so that I can say with conviction: my life is not my own.

AWAITING YOUR RETURN

Where can I go from your Spirit?
Or where can I flee from your presence?
If I ascend to heaven, you are there;
If I make my bed in Sheol, behold, you are there.

PSALM 139:7-8 NASB

Praise the Lord that He is relentless in pursuing our hearts. Although we clothe ourselves with immorality, he clothes us with righteousness. He gently whispers "Go and sin no more," with such tenderness, and he is longing, waiting to pour out mercy. He is patiently waiting with a smile, calling to us when we hide, "I just want to be merciful to you. I just want all of your heart. I just want you. I am only waiting for you to return to my open arms."

Why do we replace God so easily with things so inferior to the magnificent lover that he is? Why do we rush so quickly into a tangible love yet neglect our true love? Do we simply not readily feel, see, and sense his presence? Faith is the assurance of what is hoped for and the conviction of what is not seen (Hebrews 11:6). Turning to each new love is really nothing more than a lack of faith. It is a disbelief in the ability of God to satisfy our desires. It is an abandoning of trust in Him to be our all in all, and more than enough.

Forgive me, Father. I am so quick to pursue other loves, and all along you are waiting patiently to restore me with mercy.

WILDERNESS

"I will allure her,
and bring her into the wilderness,
and speak tenderly to her."
HOSEA 2:14 ESV

Do you ever feel like God has taken you into the wilderness? We crave comfort and familiarity, but the Lord knows that sometimes in order for us to hear his heart, he must lead us out of those surroundings for a season. A comfortable life can lead us into periods of stunted growth, and it is only when he brings us into a wild and untamed place that we begin to see that there are things that need to be uprooted, trimmed off, and allowed to die in order for new growth to happen.

These seasons are not punishment. God wants us to learn to sing and hope in the valley as well as on the mountaintop. How good he is to never be content with our unholy state, but to do whatever is necessary to perfect us.

Thank you, Lord, that you will do what it takes to make sure my heart is moving ever closer to yours. It is your mercy and faithfulness that cause you to bring me to these deserts when I am comfortable with streams of water. May I never stop believing in your goodness.

PILGRIMAGE

Blessed are those whose strength is in you,
whose hearts are set on pilgrimage.
As they pass through the Valley of Baka,
they make it a place of springs;
the autumn rains also cover it with pools.
PSALM 84:5-6 NIV

As much as we may try, this world is not our home. Those who have accepted the fact that they are just passing through will be happier than those who are convinced that all of life's fulfillment must be found within this lifetime. The Valley of Baka in Psalm 84 is translated as the Valley of Tears. We all walk through a proverbial valley of tears sometime in our lives, but those who have set their hope on the Lord will see the hardships of this life as growth possibilities. They will be capable of turning their tears into fortitude to meet the challenges in the valleys. They will set their faith on the strength of the Lord to carry them through.

Can you envision this life as a pilgrimage that will lead to your final destination in heaven? Alternatively, do you see life as a one-shot chance to get everything right, to do all that you want, and to capitalize on success in this lifetime only?

Lord, help me remember that my hope cannot be tied to everything going right in my life but set on you alone.

LONELINESS

Those who look to him for help will be radiant with joy;
no shadow of shame will darken their faces.
PSALM 34:5 NLT

Do you ever let loneliness define you? We all have seasons
of loneliness, even in the midst of intimate relationships.
Marriage can be lonely when you feel like you're not
communicating well. Motherhood can be lonely when you
feel like you're the only one dealing with certain issues.
Friendships can be lonely when you feel misunderstood.
If you are not careful, you can get into a season when you
let loneliness define you. When that happens, ask yourself,
"Where have I set my eyes?"

When your gaze is on the Lord you will have a joyfulness
that you did not possess previously. God has given you
abundant life, so why should you live as if the world
is falling apart? Even though your circumstances are
challenging, God's character has not changed. Your role is
to properly respond to his character in all situations; that is
the heartbeat of the Christian life.

God, loneliness is hard, but I know it does not define me.
When I feel overwhelmed by loneliness, please help me to
keep my gaze set on you. You will give me joy even when
times are painful.

COMPASSION IN OUR CRYING

LORD, answer me because your love is so good.
Because of your great kindness, turn to me.
PSALM 69:16 NCV

Sometimes we cry out to the Lord for days, weeks, or years regarding a specific trial, but we seem to receive no answer. This can be disheartening, but it will not last forever. Because of his great love and compassion, he will hear our cries and turn his face of blessing toward us. Verse 33 of this psalm says he listens to his own and those in need.

Even if God is quiet, we should continue to praise him and give him thanks. Even in pain and before we are rescued (v. 30) we can glorify God. Our rescue from a situation or a heartache is not the thing that we seek the most; the Lord is what we want more than anything, even our own desires.

Lord, I can feel so alone when you are quiet as I cry out. Help me know that you hear me, and because of your kindness and love you will answer me and provide the rescue at the right time. I trust you, Jesus.

FORGIVENESS

Be kind to one another, tenderhearted,
forgiving one another, as God in Christ forgave you.
EPHESIANS 4:32 ESV

We know we are called to forgive one another, but do we ever try to maintain a heart of forgiveness toward someone who repeatedly offends us? How do we continually forgive someone when there is no sign of change in the person's actions? The answer lies in Christ's forgiveness of us.

When we consider the kindness and grace of God toward us it becomes difficult to hold on to bitterness. His repeated offer of mercy to us, when we truly acknowledge and embrace it, makes it nearly impossible to be unforgiving of others. If we find ourselves struggling to forgive someone who has hurt us time and again, we need to check to see if we have truly accepted the forgiveness of Christ in our own lives. His mercy allows us to be merciful.

God, help me fully understand the gravity of my sin and your forgiveness. I sin over and over again, and yet you are faithful to forgive me each time. May that same mercy overtake me when I consider those in my life who need to be forgiven.

CARED FOR

He is our God,
and we are the people of his pasture
and the sheep of his hand.
PSALM 95:7 NASB

For many of us, we are responsible for the care of others, whether it's children who cannot take care of themselves, employees who need our guidance, or fellow students who need encouragement in a group project. It can feel like everything rests on our shoulders and if we fail to step up, projects, people, or companies will collapse.

That is a big weight to carry, whether the responsibility is perceived or real. It is easy to forget that we are not our own caretakers. We have a God who faithfully cares for us. Not everything depends on us even when we feel like it does. It is okay to step back, let something go undone, admit our need, and allow God to shepherd our hearts. He sees all that we are responsible for, and he will care for our soul and our physical needs.

God, you care for me. What a relief to know that not everything depends on me doing everything; you will handle all the things that I cannot, and you take pleasure in providing for me. May I rest in that knowledge today.

A PEACEFUL MIND

You will keep in perfect peace
those whose minds are steadfast,
because they trust in you.
ISAIAH 26:3 NIV

Many of us wake up in the middle of the night and consider all the things that we need to get done in the day ahead. Those anxiety-inducing nights leave us exhausted and wishing we had a switch so we could turn off our minds. Worry can cripple us, but God already has remembered every detail, so why should we become slaves to that to-do list?

God's love for us ensures that he will take care of every little detail in our lives. He loves to provide for us in ways that we might consider too small for him. The next time we find ourselves becoming anxious about all the things that must be done or worrying that we will forget something, we need to steady our hearts with the knowledge that God cares about the infinitesimal details of our lives.

God, when I start to worry, help me remember that you are not forgetful. You do not overlook things, and you can be trusted to provide for me in the big and small details of life. May my heart and mind be at peace in you.

HIS HOUSE

Blessed are those who dwell in your house!
They are ever praising you.
PSALM 84:4 NASB

If you find yourself dissatisfied lately, ask yourself whose house you've been dwelling in. You were never meant to engage yourselves so fully in the pursuits of the world that you forget to pursue the things of the Lord. Have you forgotten to partake in true and meaningful worship beyond only Sunday mornings? Have you made your goals a priority in your life, letting the goals of sanctification and loving Jesus slide to the back of your mind? Have you involved yourself in so many other activities that spending quality time in the Word rarely happens anymore?

If you have been residing in your own house, metaphorically, you will eventually find yourself dissatisfied. Check your heart, consider your priorities, and see if you need to come back to the house of the Lord. His doors are open, and he will welcome you in with joy.

It is so easy to get caught up in my own goals and pursuits, even if they are good things. Forgive me, Jesus, and help me come back to your house where I engage in worship, thankfulness, and simply loving you and being loved by you.

Through the Sea

Your way was through the sea,
your path through the great waters;
yet your footprints were unseen.
PSALM 77:19 ESV

God's way often looks confusing to us. Why would he lead his people through the sea instead of across dry land? Why would he lead us through infertility, loss, heartbreak, or sickness? He leads us into places where, on our own, we may very likely fail or get swept away by the raging emotions and tumultuous waves of pain and confusion.

God does this to remind us of our limited understanding and his omniscience, our delicacy and his tender care, our incompetence and his omnipotence. If his way is leading through the sea, passing by the dry land, there's a lesson in trust to find the best possible route. God can walk on water and part those seas; he's got us covered.

God, there are easier ways to get through this life, but please help me understand that I only know in part and can't see all that you are doing. Help me trust you even when I do not fully comprehend your ways.

BEAUTY

The heavens declare the glory of God;
and the firmament shows his handiwork.

PSALM 19:1 NKJV

It's good to be reminded of God's beauty. In our busy lives we might not notice the wonder that surrounds us, but all of it points to the glory of God. Nature is a testimony to God's amazing beauty. His character is lovely; his sacrifice on the cross is glorious; and his grace is seen in every changed heart. We only need to look around. His glory is shown in the rising sun, in the little faces that look up at ours, and in the way he speaks to our hearts to refresh and transform us.

It's rejuvenating to notice his beauty today. It's refreshing to observe his glory while outside under the great sky. It's invigorating to notice the work that God is doing in the hearts of people around us. It allows us to consider our lives and the way God transforms us. We give thanks for the beauty of his character. We praise him for his kindness, grace, justice, and love. Today is a good day to notice God's beauty.

Lord, your glory fills the earth. Forgive me for failing to notice it regularly. Help me notice and give thanks for the beautiful creation that surround me.

LACKING NO GOOD THING

For the Lord God is a sun and shield;
the Lord bestows favor and honor;
no good thing does he withhold
from those whose walk is blameless.

PSALM 84:11 NIV

Perhaps you woke up today feeling entitled to certain things in your life. You work hard, you love Jesus, you sacrifice so that God can be glorified, and others can see his goodness. But sometimes all of that leaves you feeling that you have earned the right to certain things: a break, ease and comfort, or a nicer house, perhaps?

If you are struggling with entitlement and wondering why some people have things that you lack, then you need this reminder: no good thing does he withhold from those whose walk is blameless. No good thing. None. God bestows on his righteous ones all that they need. Instead of focusing your attention on what you think you lack, focus instead on loving the Lord and giving thanks to him for all that he does provide. If it is good for you, he will give it to you!

God, forgive me for seeing all that I lack instead of giving thanks for all that you have already given me. I lay at the cross these feelings of entitlement, and I choose to live today with thankfulness in my heart.

Growing in Dry Seasons

Let us not grow weary of doing good,
for in due season we will reap, if we do not give up.
Galatians 6:9 esv

Despite the lack of rain, the stubborn vines wove their way through the cracks in the fence, taking over wooden planks and other plants alike. While everything else suffered in the drought, the weeds seemed to thrive on the lack of water. Without the care of a gardener to pull back the weeds and water the flowers, the assertive vines soon dominate the area.

In the spiritually dry seasons of our lives, it is easy for bad habits, wrong thoughts, and lies from the enemy to choke out our spiritual growth. It is imperative that we continue to keep pursuing things that we know will aid our relationship with Christ. This might be even more important when we don't feel anything or have lost the sense of his presence. Good habits, like time in the Word, corporate worship with other believers, and accountability with a close friend, will help us continue to grow and eventually pull out of the spiritual drought.

Lord, when I am struggling in my relationship with you, please help me continue to do what I know is right and good and will benefit my relationship with you. I do not want to become lazy but to press on faithfully.

TOOLS FOR EVERY SITUATION

Grace was given to each one of us
according to the measure of Christ's gift.
EPHESIANS 4:7 ESV

Have you ever been in the midst of worship, feeling
the presence and pleasure of God strongly, only to be
pulled back to the harsh reality of life on earth by an
unpleasant situation? Maybe it was your kids fighting or
your roommate complaining about you. At any rate, all
sensations of awe and glory quickly vanish while dread
and agitation roll swiftly in. You want to scream, or rebel,
or something! How rude to be interrupted in your time
with Jesus just to deal with this!

While the interruptions are annoying and unappreciated,
you must remember that you possess the tools to
overcome the situations with grace and quietude. God's
grace has been given to you according to what he knows
you need. Keep your eyes riveted on him and remember
the mercy that he shows you daily. Let that be your
example as you work with the struggling people and
difficult circumstances around you.

God, I so easily become agitated, but I know that you have
already given me what I need to deal with each situation
graciously.

EMPOWERED

You belong to God, my dear children. You have already
won a victory over those people, because the Spirit who
lives in you is greater than the spirit who lives in the world.

1 JOHN 4:4 NLT

Do you ever think to yourself that you should have more
figured out in life than you do? Perhaps it is your age, or
the number of years you've walked with the Lord, or the
expectations of the world. These milestones can cause you to
think you should be farther along in life than you seem to be.

When these thoughts overcome you, do not panic or
wonder how long you will struggle before you have life
figured out. Instead, remember you live empowered by
the Spirit of the living God. His power actually lives within
you, and you can draw on that power in your day-to-day
life. Whether you're doing the dishes, answering curious
questions, managing employees, or fixing houses, you
have been empowered for that life. It doesn't mean that
you won't ever get tired, but hopefully it means you will
not grow weary. Choose to live empowered by God for
whatever he brings your way.

Lord, remind me that you truly are omnipotent and your
power dwells within me. I am not doing life by myself, nor
am I doing it for myself, but for you alone!

RELAX

The LORD watches over the foolish;
when I was helpless, he saved me.
I said to myself, "Relax,
because the LORD takes care of you."
PSALM 116:6-7 NCV

Life can feel so defeating. Sometimes we already want to go back to bed right after we get up! The kids won't stop fighting, we've already received some bad news, and the headlines are telling another tragic story. It is hard to hold on to the promises of God's goodness when our day starts with such heaviness. We want God to give us peaceful mornings, children who are kind and obedient, and for the drama to at least wait until after we've had our coffee.

God's goodness shines through in our lives in many ways, but sometimes it takes pain, grief, and heavy circumstances before our distracted eyes can see. Sometimes he strips things away in order to give us new gifts. Sometimes our difficulties reveal his hand carrying us through the mess. So, whether our day is full of peace or it's crumbling already, we can always remember that God's got this. We can relax.

Lord, thank you that regardless of how my day starts, you are in control and your goodness will be shown to me today. I trust you with this day. You will not let me be defeated.

READY TO FORGIVE

You, Lord, are good, and ready to forgive,
and abundant in mercy to all who call upon you.
PSALM 86:5 NASB

How should we describe ourselves when it comes to holding grudges? Are we "ready to forgive and abundant in mercy?" Or is it more accurate to say that we are "quick to become angry and struggle to let go of offenses?" While we would all like to describe ourselves as the former, the latter description is possibly the tendency.

God has endured more rebellion, offense, and hate than any of us could ever imagine, yet he is still described as good, and ready to forgive. Oh, that we could abound in mercy like he does! Imagine being hurt beyond belief, but as soon as the opportunity arises to forgive, we jump on it. That is what God does for us every time we call on him in repentance. Ask God for that grace to forgive today.

Lord, I am so slow to let go of some offenses. I hold grudges and allow myself to become bitter toward people who have hurt me. Please forgive me and help me grow in mercy so that I can be ready to forgive when the opportunity arises.

THIS GOOD DAY

Satisfy us in the morning with your unfailing love,
that we may sing for joy and be glad all our days.

PSALM 90:14 NIV

"How was your day?" he asks when you get home. You respond positively that you got the promotion you were working for, or you had a great time with your girlfriends. Maybe the only truth is that the kids didn't want to kill each other for once and that's good news! How often are our good days marked by things that are pleasurable or easy for us, or by things that went the way we were hoping they would go?

When we consider a day to be good only when things go well for us, we shrink the world down to our own little kingdom of one. We make everything about us. In reality, our world extends so far beyond ourselves. We can consider even the hardest days to be good when we recognize God's hand in it. You didn't get the promotion? Thank God for his goodness regardless.

God, forgive me for making my day all about me and failing to acknowledge how you are working even when things don't go my way. I see this day as good even if all goes wrong.

Only One Rescuer

Lord, I have come to you for protection;
don't let me be disgraced.
Save me and rescue me,
for you do what is right.
PSALM 71:1-2 NLT

Do you ever notice when life gets tough there are certain things you look at as an escape? Maybe it's relationships that seem better than the one you're in, or a trip to a new place where none of your current troubles exist. Maybe you look for adventures instead of the monotonous, or even a good night's sleep. All these things will not satisfy your longings, they will not rescue you from your troubles, and they will not provide you with the escape you think you need.

But do you know what will? God, your only hope, your ever-present help in times of trouble, and your strength when you are weakness. So be courageous even if courage means simply smiling through your difficulties instead of allowing weariness to cover your face. You have a beautiful inheritance as the daughter of the King. Is that not worth smiling about?

Oh Lord, help me see you as the true rescuer, the one who can satisfy my longings. When I am beginning to seek out other things to satisfy me, convict me and remind me to put my hope in you.

CRAVING CLARITY

"My thoughts are not your thoughts,
neither are your ways my ways," declares the LORD.
"For as the heavens are higher than the earth,
so are my ways higher than your ways
and my thoughts than your thoughts."

ISAIAH 55:8-9 ESV

It's a wonderful thing to have clarity. Clear-cut, easy to read, black and white instructions are highly coveted by those of us who don't like to guess. We are possibly the ones who read the Bible as if it is an instruction manual. We look for the to-dos and the lists in the Word so life can be easily understood. Even if this doesn't fully describe us, it's unlikely that we crave the opposite—living in complete obscurity without any clear direction. Much of life is confusing, but fortunately for us we are not left to our own resources as we walk through our days.

As children of God, we are connected by grace to the One who is never confused, never unsure of what to do next, and has never lost control. This means that we do not need to live in fear of uncertainty. We have a guide who will lead us with perfect faithfulness and will provide all the grace we need for each day.

Lord, may I never make clarity an idol in my life. I do not need to understand what is happening; I just need to trust the One who does. May I lean on you instead of my own insight today?

CUT OUT FOR THIS

God chose the foolish things of the world to shame the
wise, and he chose the weak things of the world
to shame the strong.

1 CORINTHIANS 1:27 NCV

Do you struggle to feel "cut out" for what God has called
you to do in this season? Most of us don't feel sufficiently
prepared at various points in our lives. But here is a
reminder in today's verse. God uses the weak to shame the
strong, and he has you exactly where you need to be. He
has placed you amongst those you need to be with, and
you are doing what you need to be at this time in your life.

Simple obedience and courageous willingness are all the
Lord needs from you today. You don't need wisdom or
talent or a more intriguing personality. He knew exactly
who you were when he called you, with all your quirks
and foibles. He is not surprised or disappointed with who
you've turned out to be. You are enough in him. Rejoice
that he will use you today.

God, thank you that you have called me to this life. While
I do not feel adequate for it sometimes, your power in me
and your grace for me are sufficient. Help me trust that I
am exactly where I need to be.

DECLARATIONS

It is good to give thanks to the LORD,
and to sing praises to your name, O Most High;
to declare your lovingkindness in the morning,
and your faithfulness every night.

PSALM 92:1-2 NKJV

If there is one practice that can totally change our outlook on life, it is that of giving thanks. Acknowledging the goodness, faithfulness, and provision of God will turn covetousness into contentment, and angst into anticipation. God comes through reliably and regularly and often our selfishness stops us from seeing all that is good.

How did you start your day today? Was it in joyful worship, declaring the lovingkindness of God? Or was it with anxiety, irritation, or complacency? Beginning each day with declarations of all that you are thankful for will ensure that you enter into the rest of your day with a peace-filled, happy heart. Likewise, ending your day by giving thanks to God for the way he faithfully led you through it will help you see all that went well instead of all that went wrong. Challenge yourself to give thanks morning and night this week and see what it does for your heart.

Lord, there is so much to be thankful for. Remind me to declare your goodness day and night; you are so faithful to me!

HELPED BY MERCY

When I thought, "My foot slips,"
your steadfast love, O LORD, held me up.
When the cares of my heart are many,
your consolations cheer my soul.
PSALM 94:18–19 ESV

"If the Lord had not been my help…" How would we finish that sentence? "If the Lord had not been my help, I would have settled into a life of depression and despair." "If the Lord had not been my help, I would have given up on a difficult marriage." "If the Lord had not been my help, I would have stopped pursuing the things of God and I'd be living empty of any purpose right now." There are endless ways this thought could be completed, but thanks be to God, he has been our help!

In the times we think our feet are slipping and we won't make it out alive—or at least whole—the Lord upholds us in his mercy. God keeps us steady in his love, and he does not let us carry our burdens alone. Whatever cares weigh us down today, we only need to remember that our cares are the Lord's too. He is ready to assume our burdens, extend comfort and mercy, and give us the love that only he is capable of giving.

God, thank you that your mercy and love keep me from a life of destruction and pain. Though I stumble, your hand supports me. You are so good.

No Better

There is a path before each person that seems right,
but it ends in death.
PROVERBS 16:25 NLT

Perhaps your struggle with sin does not manifest itself in loud or glaring ways. Does this mean that you are better at being a Christian than others? Or maybe it means that you need to pay even more attention to the ways of the Lord? Those who struggle inwardly need to be hyper-vigilant. It's too easy to start believing that a brief moment of impure thoughts, or the disbelief in God's ability to provide, or harboring anger at a spouse or children isn't really *that* bad. The enemy needs only a small foothold in our hearts to begin to work his deception and cause us to think that we know better than God.

If you sense that in yourself today, run to God's throne of grace in repentance. Don't hesitate in shame. Admit your folly and your reticent sin and ask for forgiveness. Do not allow yourself to think that you know better than God. That is a sure path to destruction.

Lord, I am so humbled by your mercy when I have once again considered myself wiser than you. Help me to see my sin as the sin that it is and to not allow myself to think that any of it is acceptable.

LOOK UP

Lift up your eyes and look to the heavens:
who created all these?
He who brings out the starry host one by one
and calls forth each of them by name.
Because of his great power and mighty strength,
not one of them is missing.

ISAIAH 40:26 NIV

Have you ever noticed that the darker it is, the better you can see the stars? Can you imagine what the stars look like in the wilderness? The Israelites wandered in the desert for forty years, led by the Lord, but unfortunately neglecting him. They swayed between worshiping the almighty God with reverential awe and cursing his name while pursuing idols. It was like a perverted waltz between two lovers...or three...or four.

Sometimes the Lord leads us into the wilderness for a season. It is dry and we do complain, yet he faithfully makes his presence known to us. He doesn't always show up in pillars of cloud and fire, but he's there. When we are walking through the desert, we simply need to look up. We can see God's glorious gifts, those amazing stars, which he has bestowed on us.

Jesus, may I never be so consumed by the pain in the wilderness seasons that I stop looking for your goodness. Thank you for the gift of your love.

Never Left Helpless

I was young, and now I am old,
but I have never seen good people left helpless
or their children begging for food.
PSALM 37:25 NCV

Kaylee received bad news from her husband: their loan payments were coming due and were much higher than expected. Where would the money come from? She panicked, wondering what they could cut from their budget in order to make room for this higher monthly expense. As is common to us in these scenarios, anxiety consumed her.

When things like this happen, it is easy to become overwhelmed. We know from experience that worrying does nothing to help the situation, and yet it is hard not to. But when has God ever forsaken us in our need? Has he not always come through for us with complete faithfulness? There are better places for our energies than to give ourselves over to anxious thoughts. We can release anything that is troubling us to God today and focus our minds on his faithfulness.

Lord, how many times have I allowed worry to dictate my moods and responses? Forgive me for so quickly forgetting that you have been faithful to care for your righteous ones. I need not worry!

THE BEST THING

You will make known to me the way of life;
in your presence is fullness of joy;
in your right hand there are pleasures forever.
PSALM 16:11 NASB

What good things have been distracting us from the best thing? Our lives are flooded with amazing things. We have children that keep us running, homes that need to be taken care of, gardens that require tending, jobs that demand attention, and relationships that need cultivation. These are good things, necessary things. But they can also serve as distractions from the very best thing—time with Jesus.

Psalm 16 tells us that in the presence of God is fullness of joy. Not just some joy, but complete joy. In his right hand are pleasures forever. When we neglect to make time in our busy lives for the best thing, we are cheating ourselves out of complete joy and eternal pleasure. Sounds like a bit of a waste, right? Be encouraged today to set aside something good in order to make time for the very best.

Lord, my life is full of so many good gifts, but I realize that I tend to treat them as distractions from the very best thing. Help me to not neglect time with you for the sake of completing my to-do list.

CALLED TO FAITHFUL LIVING

Blessed is the one who perseveres under trial because,
having stood the test, that person will receive the crown
of life that the Lord has promised to those who love him.

JAMES 1:12 NIV

When we are young and ambitious, we like to think of
all the exciting things we'll do with our lives—travel,
start a business, bring change to our government, find a
spouse, and make a beautiful life together. The thrill of the
unknown excites and motivates us.

As we get older, we realize that life is more about
faithfulness than thrills. All the wonderful plans require
effort and perseverance. These things do not happen
overnight. But a life of faithfulness is no less worthy
of a calling than a life of adventure and excitement.
Sometimes God takes us into seasons when perseverance
is needed daily. But when we make the choice to remain
faithful in our jobs, our homes, our relationships, and
especially our obedience to Christ, we are setting
ourselves up for a wonderful reward in the age to come.

God, thank you for the opportunity to remain faithful to
you even when life isn't as exciting as I anticipated. Help
me to wake up every day and choose to do what is right in
your eyes so I can please you.

LOVE WHAT IS GOOD

You who love the LORD, hate evil!
He protects the lives of his godly people
and rescues them from the power of the wicked.
PSALM 97:10 NLT

Here's a challenging question. Do we hate evil, or are we justifying some things that are not pleasing to God? Psalm 97 says that those who love the Lord will hate evil, but do we really? Do we tolerate some choices or behaviors and make excuses for them and then claim them as "not that bad?"

God's protection and his rescue are benefits for his faithful ones. Christians should love what is good and set aside things that do not align with God's ways. We don't want to miss out on those things! We need to take a deep look at our lives today to ensure that we are walking in righteousness and not making room for evil things in our hearts and our minds.

God, I am guilty of letting things in my life that I know are not pleasing to you. Please forgive me! Help me to see things as they really are—evil as evil and righteous as righteous. Let me not deceive myself!

MADE FOR CONNECTION

Exhort one another every day,
as long as it is called "today," that none of you
may be hardened by the deceitfulness of sin.
HEBREWS 3:13 ESV

God has given us so many sweet things as his children. One of his greatest gifts is that of community. God didn't create us to do life all on our own. If we think back to the Garden of Eden, he created Adam and Eve so they would have each other! But how often do we isolate ourselves and then struggle through the hard times in life?

We were made to live with each other as the body of Christ. Our church is for connecting, holding one another accountable, and encouraging each other in our walks with the Lord. When we keep ourselves away from those friendships with other believers, we find lies easier to believe, we feel alone in our struggles against sin, and we think that nobody cares about us. Nothing could be further from the truth. Let's challenge ourselves to initiate a conversation with a sister in Christ today. Let's see how we can build each other up in the Lord.

Lord, sometimes it feels easier to keep to myself, but I know that's not what you made me for. Help me be bold in looking for ways to connect with other believers so that I can continue to grow the way you intended.

SEPTEMBER

A desire accomplished
is sweet to the soul,
But it is an abomination
to fools to depart from evil.

PROVERBS 13:19 NKJV

REJOICE

Rejoice in the Lord, you righteous,
and give thanks at the remembrance of his holy name.
PSALM 97:12 NKJV

We will always be able to find reasons to stop rejoicing. Things will always be more difficult than we anticipated; things will always disappoint us. If rejoicing came easily, it probably wouldn't be a repeated command in Scripture! God knew that with all the difficulties in life, finding joy in the Lord would need to be a daily choice—or maybe even an hourly choice! If we wait until things are good enough before we rejoice, then there will always be a reason not to.

Are you choosing gladness in your heart today despite circumstances that are less than perfect? Take a moment now to give thanks, if not for anything in your current situation, then for the goodness of who God is. The remembrance of his name is enough reason to give thanks and to rejoice, which is the beautiful message in today's verse. Take heart, friend, and choose joy today.

Lord, since you walked on earth, I know you can sympathize with my weaknesses and difficulties in choosing to rejoice. But I love you, Lord. I know that you are good and worthy of thanks even when I am struggling with other things. Help me rejoice today.

HIS BEST

They were completely amazed and said again and again,
"Everything he does is wonderful."
MARK 7:37 NLT

"I just want to do something well," we say in distress.
No one wants to feel like they can't give their best, but
sometimes we are stretched so thin that that is exactly
how we end up feeling. When we feel this way there are
two things to remember.

First, God is pleased with us even when we don't feel
accomplished. He is never exasperated with us because of
our lack of skills or experiences. And second, even when
we are not able to give our best, God is giving his best. He
does all things well. He is able to take our weak efforts and
turn them all into gold. It is not about performing well; it's
about God receiving all the glory and honor. He will show
himself powerful when we are anything but. Press into
him today, friend. Rest in the knowledge that even when
we can't give all that we want to, he will show up and be
all that we need him to be.

God, I am showing up today and giving all I can, but I
know it could be better. Thank you that you don't judge
me based on what I do—you see my heart and love it.

ENTITLED TO NOTHING

He has not punished us as our sins should be punished;
he has not repaid us for the evil we have done.
PSALM 103:10 NCV

What we deserve from God and what he gives us are so
vastly different. He gives mercy instead of judgment;
eternal life instead of eternal separation; and good gifts
instead of punishment. When we are tempted to think
that God is being unfair or life is unjustly difficult, we can
also remember that everything in our lives is grace.

We are not entitled to a certain kind of life. We have
no right to ease, comfort, or fulfilled dreams. Every
good thing in our lives is because of the mercy that
God bestowed upon us. The only thing we earned was
punishment and death. If the world and the flesh are
tempting us to feel that life shouldn't be so hard, we only
need to remember: "For by grace you have been saved
through faith; and this is not of yourselves, it is the gift
of God; not a result of works, so that no one may boast"
(Ephesians 2:8-9).

Lord, when I start to feel entitled to things, please help
me remember that everything I have is because of your
abundant grace and mercy. Thank you!

Harvest

Consider it all joy, my brothers and sisters, when you encounter various trials, knowing that the testing of your faith produces endurance. And let endurance have its perfect result, so that you may be perfect and complete, lacking in nothing.

JAMES 1:2-4 NASB

Christie's kids came to her in a panic: "Mom!" they cried, "your potato plants are dying!" They were right. While everything else in the late summer garden was flourishing with thick, green foliage and heavily laden with fruit, the potato plants' leaves were yellow and wilted—a sure sign of the end of their life. What her kids didn't know was that underneath the soil the potatoes were just fine, finishing their growth before a bountiful harvest.

Life is like that sometimes, too. There are times when it looks like things aren't going well. We're certain that means no fruit from all the effort we've put in, but underneath, God is doing things that we can't see. In the end there will be a harvest beyond our wildest imaginations. What kind of harvest are you working toward today?

God, when things aren't turning out the way I expected, help me remember that you are working in ways that I may not be able to see. Help me persevere and reap a harvest of righteousness and faithfulness.

REST

He said, "My Presence will go with you,
and I will give you rest."
EXODUS 33:14 NKJV

Rest is undervalued and difficult to find. The world touts busyness as if it were a prize. "How are you?" people ask us. And we always answer, "Busy!" We don't take our necessary rest because culture tells us we're doing something wrong if life isn't full of activity. We don't rest because we feel lazy when we do. We don't rest because we fear that things will go wrong if we aren't doing work. We don't rest because we want to prove ourselves capable.

But God wants rest for us. He honors it. He knows that keeping ourselves running at full steam will not serve us well; it is rest with him that restores us. It's true that things might go undone. People might look at us oddly when we don't cram our schedules full. It will take some getting used to. But soon we will find that when we set aside time to honor God and fulfill our need for rest, we will feel refreshed, we will avoid burn out, and our lives will be full of peace.

God, help me learn to rest, especially in your presence. I want my life to be marked by peace, not by a full schedule.

DESPERATION

"If he cries out to me for help,
I will listen, because I am merciful."
EXODUS 22:27 NCV

Desperation is an unwanted companion in many seasons of life, and, as evidenced in the Psalms, a common emotion throughout history. God does not tire of our desperate cries, though. His compassion causes him to incline his ear toward us when we cry in desperation. He doesn't shut the door on us like an aggravated parent whose child won't stop crying. Instead, he is patient and gracious with us in our messy, despondent state.

It's okay to cry out to the Lord in desperation. We don't have to feel the need to pull ourselves together to present to anyone a picture-perfect daughter of God. We can be patient with ourselves as we keep crying out, and we know that the Lord will listen because of his mercy.

God, I don't like feeling desperate because I want to be capable and self-sufficient. You don't need me to be that way though. You are okay with my ugly cries and my broken heart. Thank you for listening. May I know your presence and comfort in the midst of my desperation.

HOPE OF RESTORATION

The LORD will give what is good,
and our land will yield its increase.
PSALM 85:12 ESV

We need to understand something as followers of God. Right now, things in the world are not as they should be. Life is difficult, messy, and troublesome. Relationships are broken and much more work than we anticipated. Our efforts are met with disappointments. It sounds depressing, but we have to remember that we are not living just for life in this world.

The Scriptures paint beautiful pictures of what life will be like when God restores his creation. Not only do we have eternity to look forward to, but he gives us tastes of the glory and hope which is to come. Our lives will be marked by faithful and righteous living. He will provide what is good. He will restore our relationships. He will wipe away our tears. As hard as today may be, do not lose hope that the Lord will restore all things.

Lord, while life is a struggle now, may I not give up hope that you will bring complete restoration someday. Help me walk in faithfulness to you, knowing that you are faithful to me.

UNCONDITIONAL

The mountains may be removed and the hills may shake,
but my favor will not be removed from you,
nor will my covenant of peace be shaken,"
says the LORD who has compassion on you.
ISAIAH 54:10 NASB

Shana would be the first to admit that her ability to love was pretty shaky. Her spouse and her children knew that, while she did her best to follow God's example of loving unconditionally, Shana really did impose conditions for her love to be kind, calm, or patient. Perhaps you can relate.

God's love for us is really nothing like the love we experience with each other. It doesn't matter what happens in the world or in our lives, his love for us is guaranteed; nothing can shake it. God's love is not based on what we do. It is based on his compassionate character and his covenant, so we know it is completely secure! Every day we can thank him for the certainty of his love. We can ask him to empower us to love as he does.

Lord, as much as I hate to admit it, I know that my love has conditions. Help me learn to love as you do. Your love is full of compassion and regards me with favor despite my faults and mistakes. I want to love like that!

GROWING WITH GOD

Just as you received Christ Jesus as Lord, continue to live your lives in him, rooted and built up in him, strengthened in the faith as you were taught, and overflowing with thankfulness.

COLOSSIANS 2:6-7 NIV

What are you doing to root your life in Christ? Calling yourself a Christian or attending church now and then will not be enough. In order to sustain your walk with God in a world that is constantly pulling at your heart and drawing your mind towards other things, you need certain habits. You need daily choices which will root you in him. These choices will go a long way toward the effort to live your life in God. The world sees God as the enemy, and the flesh seek to drag you away.

Take a look at your life now and ask yourself if you are established in things which allow you to be built up in Christ. This might mean being part of a community of believers who provide encouragement and accountability. God desires to do this life with you; make sure you are doing life with him.

Lord, it is so easy to fall into habits that do not support a growing life with you. Help me fill my life with things that will establish and build up my walk with you.

PLEASURE IN WEAKNESS

I take pleasure in my weaknesses, and in the insults, hardships, persecutions, and troubles that I suffer for Christ. For when I am weak, then I am strong.
2 CORINTHIANS 12:10 NLT

The apostle Paul had a long list of hardships which he took pleasure in for the sake of knowing God's strength in his weakness. His list is probably more extreme than one you or I could come up with, but nonetheless, we are all faced with troubles and weaknesses that make daily life challenging. The intensity of someone else's troubles does not negate the difficulty of what you face, so take a moment today to make your own list of things that you choose to take pleasure in for the sake of Christ as you find his grace sufficient for you.

You may take pleasure in your weaknesses in the areas of solo parenting, sick babies, the continual sacrifice of sleep, loss of control over work issues, travel plans changing, stress at school, or marriage pressures. Because of Christ, when you are weak, you are strong.

God, it is hard to take pleasure in the things that cause me to feel weak, but I know that you give grace for each of these things, so I can boast in your strength.

PERFECT FAITHFULNESS

Lᴏʀᴅ, you are my God;
I will exalt you and praise your name,
for in perfect faithfulness
you have done wonderful things,
things planned long ago.

Iꜱᴀɪᴀʜ 25:1 ɴɪᴠ

Consider for a moment the perfect faithfulness of the plans of God. God's plans have never had a glitch, an "oops," or a plan B. In the course of history over thousands of years and in generations of broken people, his plan has never gone off course. What a miracle! So, while our plans can hardly make it through a day without needing adjustment, we dwell within the hands of a God whose plans have never once messed up. Therefore, it only makes sense to submit our lives to him and trust that we are safe in his hands, even when things don't go as we expect.

Today, it is safe to say that we will likely have our plans change. How will we respond? Will we allow frustration to rise up, or will we exalt and praise the name of God because he knows exactly what he is doing?

God, when things don't go as I plan, help me trust that your plan is still at work. You are in control, you have my best interests in mind, and you are good. I can praise you, knowing this is always the truth.

WONDERFUL LOVE AND MERCY

Praise the LORD.
His love to me was wonderful
when my city was attacked.
PSALM 31:21 NCV

Have you ever experienced the mercy and love of God in an astounding and wonderful way? Jessica did on her way home from work one night when she encountered something she never thought possible. In typical rush hour traffic, she had her first real experience with extreme road rage from a stranger. She was miraculously spared harm by a bystander who intervened in the situation. She was overcome by shock which slowly melted into overwhelming feelings of thankfulness for the mercy and protection of God.

Sometimes God's love quietly sustains us; sometimes he blows us away with marvelous mercy. Whatever you are experiencing in your life today, praise him for it.

God, I know I don't deserve any of your love. I am humbled that you consider me a worthy receptor of your goodness and mercy. May I never take it for granted, and may I never stop boasting about it! I choose to gratefully acknowledge all the ways I experience you.

PROMISES

He has granted to us his precious and magnificent promises, so that by them you may become partakers of the divine nature, having escaped the corruption that is in the world on account of lust.

2 PETER 1:4 NASB

As followers of Christ, we have access to a source of hope and encouragement that no one else has: the promises of God. Regardless of current circumstances, life does not need to be ruled by discouragement. Instead, we can read about the promises of God and find grace and encouragement to press through all of our trials.

What is true as a daughter of God? We can declare those truths, aloud, each of us to ourselves. We are each a child of God. Only goodness and mercy will follow us. We have all we need for a complete life of godliness. We have been called by God's glory and goodness. God is with us and will help us. God's love will not be removed from us. We have the promise of eternity with Jesus. When we speak these truths to ourselves, we take hold of the hope promised to us by God himself.

God, when discouragement overcomes me, help me remember to know your promises. This life is not all there is. I have so much to look forward to in eternity. Give me the right perspective for these momentary light afflictions.

Nothing to Do with You

God our Savior revealed his kindness and love, he saved us, not because of the righteous things we had done, but because of his mercy. He washed away our sins, giving us a new birth and new life through the Holy Spirit.

TITUS 3:4-5 NLT

It really has nothing to do with you. That can feel insulting, but it is also a great relief! It doesn't matter if you have perfect church attendance, or if you have never gone to church ever. It doesn't matter if you yell at your kids every day or if you are a gentle, positive parent. It has nothing to do with what you have or have not done. Your salvation is entirely dependent upon the mercy of God.

This can be hard to accept since our society is so performance driven. But how wonderful is a gift that we have done nothing to earn and can never repay? Let the mercy of God humble you today as you think about your salvation. God loves you because he deemed you worthy of love. Do not argue with that fact. Simply open your heart to him with thankfulness.

God, thank you that your salvation is a gift and not something I have to earn. I am humbled that you would choose me to be an object of your mercy. May I also extend that mercy to people in my life.

STRENGTH FOR TODAY

Those who hope in the LORD
will renew their strength.
They will soar on wings like eagles;
they will run and not grow weary,
they will walk and not be faint.

ISAIAH 40:31 NIV

You might not be soaring on wings like eagles right now. You might not be running without growing weary. Perhaps you're barely walking, and you're certainly feeling faint. The stages of life ebb and flow, and just as winter sometimes lasts too long, sometimes a season of weariness lingers also.

If you are feeling particularly worn down, ask the Lord for new strength. Sit before him, set your distractions aside, and wait for the Lord to provide strength. His strength will come even if it is just to walk with you along the path before you. Don't get down on yourself if you are not running or flying yet; those days will come. Take the strength he gives you to walk through today. Accept the new mercy, the sufficient grace, and the divine power. They are yours in Christ Jesus.

Lord, thank you for giving me strength enough for today. Help me to continually find rest in you, setting aside the things that drain the life and energy out of me.

RICHES OF GRACE

In him we have redemption through his blood,
the forgiveness of our wrongdoings,
according to the riches of his grace.

EPHESIANS 1:7 NASB

Ella is familiar with the riches of God's grace. She lived several years in rebellion against God, pursuing worldly passions and temporary pleasures. She feels the weight of grace which drew her into the fold of God.

God's grace isn't wimpy. It doesn't cover only minor sins, it doesn't run out after an allotted period of time, and it doesn't discriminate against certain kinds of people. Perhaps that is why Paul described it as rich. It is not lacking; it is there in abundance for God's children. And just when you think God won't extend anymore, "he gives more grace" (James 4:6). So, accept it gracefully regardless of how far and how long you've run from God. His redemption is ready for you.

God, thank you that your grace does not run out. I do not have to fear going so far away from you that your grace cannot redeem me. May I walk in humble submission to your ways, understanding the riches of your grace both today and every day.

INTENTIONAL PURSUIT

I will walk with integrity of heart
within my house;
I will not set before my eyes
anything that is worthless.
PSALM 101:2-3 ESV

The righteous person understands the importance of pursuing what is good by intentionally seeking the things of God and not just letting life "happen" to them. What happens when we are not intentional with the things we spend time on, set before our eyes, listen to, and meditate upon? It is then that the things of the world begin to guide us. This is what the psalmist called "worthless" (v. 3).

Are you walking with integrity everywhere, even where no one else sees? Are you pondering things which are blameless? Are you striving to set aside anything that is impure or misrepresents the Lord? God's Word is clear about what things we should be pursuing. If you do not have clarity on what it is to seek the things of God, spend some time studying the books in the Bible written by the apostle Paul to the various churches. God did not leave us wondering how to live a holy life!

God, help me to intentionally seek things that will help me to grow as a follower of you. May I not become lazy and fall into the habits of the world. Holy Spirit, guide me!

LED BY FAITHFULNESS

You have made me see troubles,
many and bitter,
you will restore my life again;
from the depths of the earth
you will again bring me up.

PSALM 71:20 NIV

Here is a promise which can sustain us through troubling times: it is the Lord's faithfulness that brings us hard times. The Word tells us that this movement of the Lord's is for our sanctification. It's to give us a greater understanding of God's character and a way to deepen our faith. It offers an avenue to awaken us when we are stagnant, and even sometimes as a way to display God's power. But it is also his faithfulness that leads us back out of those troubles.

When we understand that God hasn't left us, it makes the hard days, weeks, or months a little sweeter. God does not delight in our troubles, and he doesn't leave us in them forever either. The psalmist declared what he knew to be true for himself: God would restore his life and bring him out of the depths. If God has brought us into the depths, we can be assured that he will bring us out of them again. He is too faithful to leave his loved ones in bitter times.

God, knowing that you are with me and that you will restore me causes my heart to hope even though my circumstances are difficult.

MIRACLES ALL AROUND

My whole being, praise the LORD.
LORD my God, you are very great.
You are clothed with glory and majesty.
PSALM 104:1 NCV

Sandra would normally have missed the intricacy of a spider's web which was glistening with dew in the morning light. It was her daughter, moving at her unhurried pace, who noticed it. She would not walk away until her mom had given the beautiful web its proper admiration. Children have a unique way of reminding us of the glory in creation. They notice the miracles all around us that adults so often miss because of busy lives and a multitude of distractions.

Psalm 104 details for us the wonderful things that God created. Let us not forget the beauty and glory that surrounds us daily. Let's make it a goal to get outside today and notice the miracles around us. Let's give thanks for the wonders in God's creation and remember that just as he holds the created world together, so too he holds our miraculous lives together.

God, forgive me for failing to see the glory that surrounds me because I am too consumed with my own concerns. Help me see your creation as the miracle it is and to give praise to the One who made it all with astounding excellency.

ALIVE

God, being rich in mercy, because of his great love with
which he loved us, even when we were dead in our
wrongdoings, made us alive together with Christ (by grace
you have been saved).

EPHESIANS 2:4-5 NASB

Here is a challenge: consider where you came from so
you can contemplate the glory and goodness of where
you are now. Believers can get stuck in our walks with
Christ because we see only where we are messing up and
falling short. But God doesn't just see our faults; he doesn't
see us as dying women. You and the rest of us in Christ
are no longer children under wrath who only follow the
inclinations of the flesh. We are all now alive in Christ, filled
with the Spirit, and sustained by grace for every day and
every situation.

We should not see ourselves as victims of the enemy's
attacks and slaves to our sinful natures. Neither are we
terminally flawed. We were saved by grace and are now
seated with Christ according to the mercy, love, and
kindness of God. Rejoice!

Lord, thank you for giving me a new life when I was caught
in my sin. Help me take ahold of the truth of my freedom
in Christ, and to live as a victor, not as one enslaved.

FEAR

"For I am the LORD your God
who takes hold of your right hand
and says to you, 'Do not fear;
I will help you.'"
ISAIAH 41:13 NIV

What fear do you need to be delivered from? Do you have the fear of being misunderstood? Are you plagued by the fear of rejection? Have you suffered from the fear of humility? Do you unnecessarily fear future trouble? The Bible tells us what not to fear: other gods, other people's fears, troubles of any sort, being disgraced, and bodily harm. Why should you not fear these things? It is because God is with you.

So, if you know that you do not need to fear these things, what do you do instead? Isaiah 8:13 says to fear the Lord of Hosts and to regard him as holy. Isaiah talked about giving God the worshipful submission, reverential awe, and obedient respect that he deserves. You will not have the time or mental capacity to give fear to other things if you are in awe of a holy God.

Lord, I am guilty of fearing so many things and failing to give you the holy fear that you deserve. Help me to focus on you. I know you are capable of saving me from anything that I would fear!

SING

Sing to the LORD a new song;
sing to the LORD, all the earth!
Sing to the LORD, bless his name;
tell of his salvation from day to day.

PSALM 96:1-2 ESV

Most of us have been in a dark place before. It can be hard to see anything good about life or even about God when our minds are trapped in negativity. But there is one thing that we can do when we feel ourselves slipping into that low place, and that is to sing. There is power in lifting our voices to God to declare his goodness, power, and faithfulness. It's hard to stay stuck in that dark place when we are singing the truth in songs and praises.

The Psalms are full of exhortations about singing to the Lord. It is no coincidence that the Psalms are also full of laments, desperate cries, and prayers for rescue. The psalmists knew some very dark places. But they found, as we do, that declaring the truth in song brings forth a joy and an overcoming spirit that cannot easily be brought down.

Lord, when I feel my spirit becoming heavy, remind me to sing. I know that it is an oft-written command for a good reason. Restore to me your hope and joy when I lift my voice in song to you.

SABBATH

My soul finds rest in God;
my salvation comes from him.
PSALM 62:1 NIV

The Sabbath is a countercultural and counter-intuitive reflection of God's grace for us in that we intentionally accomplish nothing, and God still pours out his love on us. The world practically shouts at us to do more, sell more, buy more, work more, and succeed more. But God's message from the beginning of time was to work hard and then allow rest.

God doesn't need us to work incessantly in order to love us. God doesn't need us to tick off all the things on our to-do lists. God doesn't demand success like the world demands success. Instead, he invites us to purposely do nothing. In doing so, we find that we are better off than if we had pushed through without stopping for a break. Embrace the call to rest, friend, and find yourself restored by God.

Lord, help me take the command to rest seriously. Taking a Sabbath day is almost a lost art, but I do not want its benefits to be lost on me. May I always find that when I have my rest in you as a priority, you come through for me in all the things that need to be done the rest of the week.

PERFECTION

I am sure of this, that he who began a good work in you
will bring it to completion at the day of Jesus Christ.
PHILIPPIANS 1:6 ESV

If perfection is our goal in life, we will wear ourselves out
before we get out of bed in the morning. While the world
shouts for us to better ourselves, better our lives, and
better our chances at success, the Lord tells us to give up
the goals that the world touts. What would he have us
pursue instead? Self-sacrifice.

It's not a theme that you hear much about these days.
Christ displayed self-sacrifice in a way that none of us will
ever fully replicate. He set an example and a standard
for us in order that we may grow to be more like him. He
uses the trials of daily life to purify us and cause our faith
to grow. We will likely never be perfect in the eyes of the
world, but dying to our own goals, dreams, and desires
will cause us to be made more and more into the image of
our perfect God.

Lord, thank you for giving me an example to follow in
your death on the cross. Help me, Holy Spirit, to deny
myself in order to be made more like Christ and attain the
perfection in him that he promises.

ALL ABOUT HIM

Our fathers in Egypt did not understand your wonders;
They did not remember your abundant kindnesses,
but rebelled by the sea, at the Red Sea.
Nevertheless he saved them for the sake of his name,
so that he might make his power known.
PSALM 106:7-8 NASB

If there was one group of people who should have understood God's power and faithfulness, it was the Israelites whom God rescued out of Egypt. It's amazing how quickly they forgot all that God did and turned to other gods. But are we really any different? By 6:30 a.m. when the kids are fighting, we forget pretty quickly that those same children are miracles from God.

Here's the thing though: God doesn't display his power, kindness, or faithfulness just so we'll notice and thank him. He does it because he has plans to make his power known throughout the world. What happens in our lives has less to do with us and more to do with his glory! Life isn't all about us when he is actually making things about him. When we forget his amazing attributes and make things about us, he is still going be gracious because he loves us and because his power must be made known.

Lord, help me recognize that my life has surprisingly little to do with me. I am here to praise you! May I promote your glory in all I do today.

REVEALED

Jesus Christ is the same yesterday
and today and forever.
HEBREWS 13:8 NIV

Every now and then, or pretty much daily for some of us, certain situations reveal that we are not the people we thought we were. Our patience wears thin when our buttons are being repeatedly pushed. Anger flares and a temper is revealed that we did not know we had. We become easily irritated by circumstances and people unexpectedly. Whether it is marriage, motherhood, roommates, or coworkers who provoke us, we are not as holy as we thought we were.

Praise God then that he is who he says he is! There will never be a situation which reveals him to be different from who we know him to be. We can fool ourselves into believing we are better than we actually are, but God is always fully and truly exactly who his Word says he is. What great comfort in knowing that he is the same yesterday, today, and forever!

Thank you, God, that you do not change like shifting shadows. I can trust your good and holy character with my whole heart.

CONSISTENCY

"When you pray, I will listen. If you look for me
wholeheartedly, you will find me."
JEREMIAH 29:12-13 NLT

Sometimes God feels so distant. Even for those of us who have walked with God for most of our lives, we sometimes feel like we forget how to seek him. We don't see fruit, we lack motivation, and we are confused and disoriented in our current season of life.

But there is something to be said about consistency. If we do what we know how to do, that is, if we read the Word, pray to our Lord, and worship with other believers, then the feeling of being separated from God will not last. If we consider athletes, they all get tired of training at some point. Their muscles are sore, they feel like they've plateaued, and aren't making noticeable progress. The spark and thrill of training is long gone. But they know that consistently pushing themselves will result in progress even when it seems far off. This is also true for our spiritual training, so let it be encouraging for us and keep us seeking God. He will be found!

Lord, when I am tired and lack motivation, help me seek you anyway. You promise that you will be found, so let that spur me on even when I don't feel your presence.

LIVING WORD

The fear of the LORD is the beginning of wisdom;
a good understanding have all those
who do his commandments.
His praise endures forever.

PSALM 111:10 NKJV

Callie was in disbelief that the same Bible which had been written centuries ago could still be relevant today. "There's nothing new in it," she said. "How can it still instruct and speak to our hearts?" She was starting to understand the truth of the message in Hebrews 4:12: the Word of God is alive and powerful. Callie was hearing that God's Word has the power to speak now just as it did when first written.

Following God's Word is the wisest thing we can ever choose to do. God's Word does not need to change with the times. It will always provide the truth that mankind needs: we are sinners in need of a heart-rescue. God, in his mercy, provided a way to do just that. It is pure joy to spend ample time in the Word. It will never go out of style, never lose its relevance, and never be wasted.

Lord, when I start to doubt the power of your Word, please remind me that my heart condition is no different from the heart conditions of the people you first came to save. We are all in need of grace, and all in need of the wisdom which your Word offers.

THE END OF YOURSELF

Jesus came to them and said,
"All power in heaven and on earth is given to me."
MATTHEW 28:18 NCV

We all have days when we feel like we have completely come to the end of ourselves. We realize that we are not as capable or self-sufficient as we thought we were. The workday was tough, the house is a disaster, the kids have too many activities, and we are emotionally disconnected from friends or loved ones. There is just too much to be done by one person!

Those end-of-your-rope moments, as uncomfortable as they are, are not to be avoided. Instead, we should embrace them. When we can't say "I got this," then we can finally realize that Jesus has got this. Our lack is always an invitation for us to remember his power and his capability. There is nothing in heaven or on earth that can hold him back or cause him to become incapable. We are in good hands. We can press into those moments and find that Jesus' power is more than enough.

Jesus, I am so thankful that you have been given all the power over every situation. Help me lean into you when my own power is clearly not enough. You are good, and I love you.

MERCY FOR ALL

They shall give thanks to the LORD for his mercy,
and for his wonders to the sons of mankind!
PSALM 107:15 NASB

If you need encouragement today, read through Psalm 107. The forty-three verses detail God's mercy which he extends to anyone who cries out to him. Our human nature tends to reserve mercy for those who do what is right, or who have repented from wrong and proven themselves worthy. But God's mercy isn't just for those who have finally gotten their act together. It is available to anyone who cries to God.

God welcomes those who are in a dark place in their lives (vv. 4-6), those who are imprisoned because of their rebellion against God (vv. 10-14), those who have lived foolishly and have brought trouble upon themselves (vv. 17-20), and those who have been caught in life's storms (vv. 23-30). No matter where you find yourself right now, whether you are walking faithfully with God or not, his mercy is available if you cry out to him.

God, thank you that I do not have to earn your mercy. May I never be too proud to admit that I need your merciful rescue. I will rejoice in your salvation and faithful love today.

OCTOBER

The LORD All-Powerful
will prepare a feast on this
mountain for all people.
It will be a feast with all
the best food and wine,
the finest meat and wine.

ISAIAH 25:6 NCV

FULLNESS OF LIFE

May you experience the love of Christ, though it is too great to understand fully. Then you will be made complete with all the fullness of life and power that comes from God.

EPHESIANS 3:19 NLT

Abundant life was something Jesus promised to us in John 10:10. The enemy seeks to destroy us at every turn with things that seem good, but Jesus' desire for us is true life that is full of his love. Why is knowing God's love so important for the Christian?

When we know how much God loves us, we can discern the lies of the enemy, trust in God's goodness even in the midst of pain, extend the same gracious love to others in our lives, and have the "fullness of life" that Ephesians 3:19 talks about. We have the wisdom, power, and unconditional love of God, and it pours through us to others. We can pray this prayer written by the apostle Paul over ourselves today, and we may truly experience all the fullness of life that comes from God.

God, I pray that you will strengthen me with your power through the Holy Spirit and that Christ will dwell in my heart through the gift of faith. May I be rooted and established in your love and come to understand it more completely so I can be filled with the fullness of life which you offer.

EMBRACING SLOW

As for me, I will look to the LORD;
I will wait for the God of my salvation;
my God will hear me.
MICAH 7:7 ESV

Sometimes we need to un-hurry our hearts. Some things slow us down throughout the day, and we would much rather not deal with them. Curious children stop and smell the flowers; our family members get sick or injured; new coworkers seem to need a lot of our help and direction. We avoid these things because we do not like delays and because our society tells us that fast is best.

But the Lord does not always work quickly. His people were enslaved in Egypt for four hundred years before he rescued them. He allowed the Israelites to wander in the wilderness for forty years before they entered the Promised Land. Judah was held captive in Babylon for seventy years before they returned to rebuild the temple. While delays are not usually in our plan, they are often part of God's. We can either join him in the shaping of our hearts or resist him.

Lord, I am often impatient when you slow me down, but help me embrace the season of slowness. May I learn to wait with you and not always be waiting for what lies beyond the delay.

MORE JESUS, LESS STUFF

Better the little that the righteous have
than the wealth of many wicked;
for the power of the wicked will be broken,
but the Lord upholds the righteous.
PSALM 37:16-17 NIV

As you shop at your local box store, open your social media apps, or talk to another mom on your kid's soccer team, you quickly begin to think that you need more and better things. Materialism is a serious addiction in our culture. God makes it clear that no matter how much you have, all of it can be stripped away at any time. It is not worth your time, attention, or resources to get caught in the trap of needing more.

What is worthy of your time and attention? Where should you put your trust and your treasure? The answer lies in the pursuit of Christ. Psalm 37 says that the Lord supports the righteous even when all they have in the eyes of the world is nothing. Walk with confidence knowing that you don't need all the new styles in order to be cared for by Christ. Look with confidence at that social media app, knowing that what you have compared to the next person doesn't matter in light of eternity.

Lord, help me to not get caught up in the cycle of filling my house and my mind with stuff, especially if I'm not filling myself with you. You are all I need.

A Soul at Rest

Return to your rest, my soul,
for the LORD has been good to you.
PSALM 116:7 NIV

Perhaps you need this reminder today: you don't need to know all the answers. You don't need to have a perfect plan in place. You don't need to spend hours every night with your anxieties, trying to solve all the problems in your life. Let your heart, mind, and soul rest. The Lord has always come through for you.

The goodness of God has never left his righteous ones abandoned with no hope. Does this mean that we do nothing about the troubles we face? No. We still act wisely, make plans, and submit them to the Lord. We use our God-given abilities to make the most of the situation at hand. But we do not let our anxieties consume us. Release to God whatever concerns you; his goodness will not leave you empty-handed.

Lord, thank you that I can entrust to you the things that concern me. When I start feeling anxious, remind me to first surrender my worries to you and then ask for your wisdom in handling the situation. Thank you that you have never forsaken your righteous one.

WHAT NEEDS TO CHANGE

God, hurry to save me;
Lord, hurry to help me!
PSALM 70:1 NASB

We have all prayed a prayer like this before: "God, hurry to help me! Save me, God!" It's not usually in the face of grave danger that we pray this, but more often because we are uncomfortable, inconvenienced, or not getting what we think we deserve. Sometimes when we cry out for a rescue, it is our mindset that needs rescued, not our circumstances.

Are we playing the victim, pitying ourselves, or complaining? It is unlikely that God will save us from the situation. He will be more likely to graciously reveal to us that our mindset needs transforming. God loves us too much to save us from the things which are meant to reveal our need for him. Instead, he will allow his Spirit to speak to our hearts and minds, bringing revelation and conviction that it is our attitude that needs to be changed. Will you hear him?

God, forgive me for crying out for rescue just because I don't like my situation. Give me your perspective so I can see that it is not my circumstances that need to change, but my heart toward the circumstances. I want to be more like you.

GREAT POWER

You will know that God's power is very great for us who believe. That power is the same as the great strength God used to raise Christ from the dead and put him at his right side in the heavenly world.

EPHESIANS 1:19-20 NCV

We tend to forget about the power that lives within us. We were never meant to struggle through life on our own. The Spirit of God dwells within us, giving us access to his wisdom and power.

What does it look like to use this power on a daily basis? It could mean we ask for wisdom before we address our disobedient child; often we'll find God gives us a creative solution which we wouldn't have thought of on our own. It could mean we ask God for an encouraging word for a friend who is struggling; the words that come from the Holy Spirit will encourage us as well! It could mean we ask God for the grace and strength to make it through a tough day; we'll realize later that he truly carried us. Inviting God to enter into these areas of our lives will remind us of the ways that his great power works in and through us. We only have to ask for it!

Thank you, Lord, for the incredible power that you have given to all believers. Help me remember that it is mine if only I will reach out and take hold of it.

GROWING HEARTS

I shall run the way of your commandments,
for you will enlarge my heart.
PSALM 119:32 NASB

One of the joys of living totally dedicated to the pursuit
of God is the satisfaction our hearts have from the pursuit
itself. The more we read the Word, study God's promises,
and follow his commands, the more we want to do it
those things all the time. Psalm 119 says that as we pursue
a life dedicated to the Lord, God will "enlarge" our hearts
to understand more and to want more of the gospel. And
as our hearts grow in love for the things of God, the things
of the world will begin to lose their appeal.

If we are constantly trying to hold on to worldly things
while also trying to keep to God's way, we will find
that we aren't as hungry for God. We are satiating our
appetites with snacks instead of waiting for the feast. If
we find ourselves unsatisfied, we can ask the Lord what
we need to surrender to him in order to go after him
wholeheartedly.

Lord, forgive me for filling up on "junk food" and not
allowing myself to be hungry for the one thing that can
truly satisfy me. Help me persist in pursuing you, and as I
do, please bring joy and genuine delight to my soul.

KNOWN AND REDEEMED

"Do not fear, for I have redeemed you;
I have summoned you by name; you are mine."
ISAIAH 43:1 NIV

Perhaps you struggle to find yourself worthy of love.
You see your flaws and your mistakes; every interaction
is another opportunity to see how you could have done
better. While you might view yourself this way, the Lord
sees you so differently. He sees you covered in mercy, not
mistakes. He sees you as one he purposely redeemed and
made his own.

You are not one whom he reluctantly brought into the
family. He knows you by name, not by your failures. He
sees you with the loving eyes of a Father which you can
only begin to comprehend as a mere mortal. Today, ask
him for those same eyes of love through which you can
see yourself. You are one who is worthy of love; you are
redeemed; you are called and known by God.

God, it can be so hard to accept my many flaws and
imperfections. I see how many times I mess up, and I
struggle to even like myself sometimes. Lord, I need your
perspective. Help me see myself through the lens of grace
through which you see me and to know the truth about
your love for me.

A Prayer for the Day

Let me hear of your unfailing love each morning,
for I am trusting you.
Show me where to walk,
for I give myself to you.
PSALM 143:8 NLT

Do your mornings start sweetly? Do you have a quiet space, a good view, and a warm cup of coffee or tea? Or are your mornings rushed and chaotic, in frustration as you leave the house? Whether your days start peacefully or with high drama, you can set yourself on a good path with this simple prayer from today's psalm: "Let me hear of your unfailing love each morning, for I am trusting you. Show me where to walk, for I give myself to you."

The psalmist asks first for a reminder of God's love. How better to start the day than by knowing you are loved? This binds your identity to the love of God. You are not identified by what you accomplish, how you act, or what others think of you. The psalm continues in prayer for direction, acknowledging that it is God who leads life. This simple surrender states that God is for you and is trustworthy regardless of how the day goes.

Lord, may I know your love and direction today. This day is yours; may your will be accomplished, not my own. You are good and I trust you!

SEASON OF FAITHFULNESS

For the word of the LORD is right and true;
he is faithful in all he does.
PSALM 33:4 NIV

If you are blessed to live in a place with changing seasons, then perhaps you are beginning to pull out cozy sweaters and long scarves. Maybe you're setting pumpkins on the porch or sipping the first pumpkin spice latte of the season. A new season is always a good time to look back on the previous one and take note of the Lord's faithfulness in your life. Doing this helps keep you alert to the ways that God is working in your life. It makes you less likely to attribute your good things or your successes to yourself.

Take time now to look back on the last few months and see how God has proven himself to be your provider and protector, as well as your source of joy and peace. Acknowledge his goodness, praise him for his leadership, and settle into fall with a determination to see his faithfulness in even greater ways.

Lord, you have been so good to me. Through the mountains and valleys of this last season you have led me with perfect faithfulness. Thank you and let me continue to recognize the ways your grace is surrounding me in this new season.

OVERFLOWING GRACE

The grace of our LORD overflowed for me
with the faith and love that are in Christ Jesus.
1 TIMOTHY 1:14 ESV

As a child, were you ever caught acting out, but your parent or teacher met that poor behavior with grace that didn't match the crime? It probably confused you, but what a relief, too! In our lives with Christ, many of our mistakes are not met with the punishment they deserve. Instead, we are given what the apostle Paul called "overflowing grace," not because we earned it, but because God is merciful.

Like one of those filling-and-dumping buckets at the kids' splash pads, God's grace is constantly pouring out on us at times when we least deserve it. It is a truth that will never get old. We cannot become numb to the Spirit's convicting power. We can never believe that we should do life all on our own. We must remain open to a life of humility and transparency. We praise God today for his overflowing grace present in our lives.

God, I feel so unworthy of your grace which just keeps coming, but I'm so very thankful that you call me worthy. May I never lose appreciation for your goodness. Keep me humble so that I never believe that I have done anything on my own to earn your love.

HELD

The LORD is close to the brokenhearted
and saves those who are crushed in spirit.
PSALM 34:18 NIV

Life is sweet, yes, but it would be naive to believe
that heartbreak will never find us even as followers of
Jesus. Whether we've walked through that pain before,
are currently going through it, or have yet to truly be
brokenhearted, there is peace to be found in this promise
from today's psalm—God is close to the brokenhearted.

What a picture of sweet love, that God draws near to those
who are hurting. When we experience pain many of us like
to be embraced by someone we love, to be brought close
and held. Even if that person cannot solve our problem
and even if they say nothing, the comfort of their presence
is such a help. In the same way, even though we cannot
see him, we know that the Lord is close to those who are
hurting. If that is you today, let the knowledge of God's
nearness bring peace to your heart.

God, thank you for drawing near to me when I am downcast.
What a comfort to know that I am held in your embrace and
do not face my pain alone.

Planting and Reaping

Those who plant in tears
will harvest with shouts of joy.
PSALM 126:5 NLT

The deep greens of summer are now transitioning into
the reds, oranges, yellows, and browns of fall as they start
to drift slowly to the ground. We are reminded again
in this season that all things in life as they start to die,
are preparing for something better. The bare trees look
death-like after months of being a beautiful living green,
but that death serves a greater purpose. The old leaves, as
they decompose on lawns and garden beds, release vital
nutrients into the soil for next year's spring growth.

Likewise in life, sometimes we are painfully preparing
for new growth and a different season through our tears
and heartaches. What feels painful enough to kill us will
prepare us for a harvest of joy when the Lord restores us
to something new and beautiful. Trust that God's work will
end, not in sorrow, but in great joy.

Lord, so many seasons of life feel like I'm losing, but I know
you are preparing me for something better. Help me trust
your process, even though the pain.

WHOLEHEARTEDLY

Give me understanding, and I shall keep your law;
indeed, I shall observe it with my whole heart.
PSALM 119:34 NKJV

To say that we'll do anything with our whole hearts is
a big statement. In a world of distractions garnering
our attentions it is difficult to focus our whole selves on
anything. But God doesn't want just part of us today and
then find us distracted with something else tomorrow.
He wants our total commitment, the same kind of
commitment he has given us which led him to the cross.
Christ must be overwhelmingly first in our lives, or
nothing. There is no in-between.

This is a huge decision to make in our lives—it is why
Jesus told us we need to take up our crosses and follow
him (Matthew 16:24). But when we set aside all other loves
and distractions, so we pursue Christ wholeheartedly, we
find a joy and sweetness in life that compares to none
other. What is distracting us from giving God our whole
hearts today?

God, I am easily distracted by the good things in this
world. Help me to truly know that none of it compares
to the joy of following you with all my heart. Pursue my
heart, God.

REPETITION

We do not lose heart, but though our
outer person is decaying, yet our inner person
is being renewed day by day.
2 CORINTHIANS 4:16 NASB

We tire of repetition, but God does not. Nature revolves around repetitive patterns. Patterns are set by our Lord around the rising and the setting of the sun, the blooming and the seeding of the plants, and the cycle of the four seasons throughout the year. Animals and humans bring their offspring into the world to start the cycle of life all over again. The repetition is not boring or lifeless; it is full of life!

God's glory is woven through all the repetitive moments of our lives, but we can miss it because it becomes mundane. Just by asking, God will open our eyes to the beauty and glory we miss because it is ordinary and repetitive. The Holy Spirit is ready to reveal himself in the little things of life as he renews our souls daily. What will we see in the ordinary things today just by having our spiritual eyes opened?

God, forgive me for overlooking the wonderful things you have created because they are repetitive. May my eyes see your glory in the small moments. Thank you that you use each day to create life in and around me.

INTENTIONAL

*"I love those who love me,
and those who seek me diligently will find me."*
PROVERBS 8:17 NKJV

When we find something we love, we make time for it even if our schedules are busy. Some people can't find the time to work out, while for those who love it, it is a priority. Some people can't find the time to read, but for others it is a joy that they will not do without. Intentionality is the key to finding the time to do something.

In our relationships with the Lord, intentionally seeking him propels us into a deeper love with him. The smallest things, when done intentionally, lead us into a relationship which we would not have otherwise. Growth happens when we choose a verse to memorize each week; or we listen to Scripture as we get ready for the day or drive the kids to school; or we choose a psalm to pray throughout the day. Meeting with God in these ordinary moments will keep us moving deeper in love with God. What can we do intentionally today to grow spiritually?

Lord, forgive me for ever thinking that I can grow in love with you without intentionally deepening my understanding of you and spending time in your Word. Help me to seek you first. You never disappoint!

ENLIGHTENMENT

I pray that your hearts will be flooded with light so that
you can understand the confident hope he has given to
those he called—his holy people who are his rich and
glorious inheritance.

EPHESIANS 1:18 NLT

We need enlightenment. We don't need some sense of
perceived reasoning or self-improvement which was the
pursuit of the high-minded thinkers in the eighteenth
century. But without God's guidance, our minds can't
grasp the incredible hope that we have as a result of
our calling into his family. We need the Spirit of God to
open our eyes in order to understand the hope we have
because we love God.

Are you living with the understanding that regardless of
what happens in your life now, you have a secure future?
Are you aware that in eternity you will be happier than
you can ever imagine? If you feel like you are living with
only a dim understanding of that hope today, ask the
Spirit to enlighten you. Ask him to flood your heart with
the knowledge that your future is saturated with hope.

Lord, I get caught up in day-to-day life, and I forget that
I have an incredible inheritance coming. May I live today
with a thorough understanding of the hope of eternity
with you.

You Have Done It

Help me, O Lord my God!
Oh, save me according to your mercy,
that they may know that this is your hand—
that you, Lord, have done it!
PSALM 109:26-27 NKJV

Often, we pray for rescue because we're a bit too self-focused. Few of us enjoy suffering or struggling, so of course it's natural to want to be saved from whatever is challenging us. But while the psalmist also prays for rescue, it isn't just for the sake of his own comfort. He's also praying that people will know what God has done and what he is capable of doing.

God does rescue because of his great love for us, yes. But he also does it because he wants his glorious name to be lifted up and made great throughout the earth. We need to check our hearts and see where our prayers for deliverance are coming from. Do we only desire our own safety or convenience or peace of mind? Or can we, like the psalmist, pray for salvation because we desire the glory of God to be revealed? "Not to us, Lord, not to us, but to your name give glory" (Psalm 115:1).

God, I desire for your glory to be made known, but maybe not as much as I desire my own comfort. Forgive me and help me make much more of you.

POWER OVER FEAR

The LORD is for me; I will not fear;
what can man do to me?
PSALM 118:6 NASB

What are you afraid of? Do you fear your spouse's disapproval? Do you fear your children's disobedience? Do you fear your friends' rejection? You can allow the fear of man to rule your heart, thereby creating a prison in your own mind; or you can remember, as the psalmist did, that because God is for you, you need not be afraid.

What is the power of man to harm or insult you compared to the power of God to save, protect, and provide? If your trust is in man, then you will fear rejection, insults, and humiliation. If you put your trust in God then you know that regardless of man's actions, God will bring you out in triumph. Choose to declare your trust in the all-powerful God today.

God, it is so easy to let myself fall into the trap of living by the fear of man. When I become caught in the cycle of fearing the negative thoughts and disapproval of those around me, please help me to remember that you are for me—I am completely protected.

WHAT YOU WORSHIP

Ascribe to the LORD the glory due his name;
worship the LORD in the splendor of his holiness.
PSALM 29:2 NIV

One struggle that Christians face today is the battle to focus
on our worship of God while not surrounded by picture-
perfect circumstances. With the advent of social media,
we have a window into everyone's homes. Unfortunately,
the highlights are what really stick with us. Now we feel
the pressure to hide our messy homes, or our imperfect
relationships, or even just our normal lives. We have exalted
perfection to a worship-worthy status, but it doesn't deserve
that spot; only the living God deserves our worship.

Do your attitudes and actions reflect that? Are you so
focused on creating Instagram-worthy homes, children,
or adventures, that you end up worshiping them instead?
When you turn your eyes from the picture-perfect lives
of social media influencers and onto Jesus, the need for
perfection fades and you can delight in knowing the one
true God. It's a joy to be known by him alone, even in the
messy, ordinary lives that we really do live.

Lord, I am guilty of being so focused on making my life
appear just right. I begin to worship the idea of perfection
instead of the perfection of you. Forgive me! You alone
deserve my praise.

HOPEFUL PROMISES

Remember your promise to me, your servant;
it gives me hope.
PSALM 119:49 NCV

Children can be persuaded to do something they don't enjoy or appreciate with a special reward. If they can have a treat after a successful grocery trip, or pizza and a movie after a day of yard work, the task is almost enjoyable. We are all incentivized by good things; they make trials and hard work more bearable.

God knew this when he gave us the promises of glory waiting for us in eternity that we find in his Word. If life has been hard lately, or if we feel the weight of a world groaning for its restoration, we simply look at the promises for God's family in his Word—the crown of life, the end of suffering and sadness, magnificent glories which we can't even begin to imagine. Our hope springs from the promises which he has made known to us, and we praise him for all of them!

Thank you, Lord, for the many promises of good things to come which you have given me in Scripture. Help me keep my mind on those promises, and not get so overwhelmed by the difficulty of my current circumstances.

ROUSED BY AFFLICTION

Teach me good discernment and knowledge,
for I believe in your commandments.
Before I was afflicted I went astray,
but now I keep your word.
PSALM 119:66-67 NASB

Have you ever taken the Lord for granted when life is calm?
When things feel stable you may feel confident in your
ability to handle what comes at you. You may assume that
it is your hard work and capabilities that are propelling you
forward in life. You may even let your heart wander and not
intentionally seek the Lord during a calm season.

Sometimes God uses painful circumstances to wake us
up and remind us that we have no real control over our
lives. Anything good that we have comes from God.
The psalmist recognized for himself that before he was
afflicted, he went astray. After he suffered, he asked for
discernment and good judgment because he realized
he needed to be led by God's Word and not by his own
capabilities. Whether facing calm or chaos, we make the
choice as to whom we will trust today.

God, help me to never think that what I have in life is
because of my own doing. Any good that I have has come
from you. Guide me by your Spirit and keep me choosing
you day after day.

ENDURING LOVE

"I love you people
with a love that will last forever.
That is why I have continued
showing you kindness."
JEREMIAH 31:3 NCV

Why does God continue showing us kindness? Why, when he is rejected, scorned, mocked, disobeyed, and stuffed into the back of the closet does he continue to love us? Even if we are not outwardly despising God, we have all preferred other things to him at some point in our lives. Likely, we still do. And yet, his love for us endures. His kindness toward us remains unaffected. His mercy streams steadily upon us like water from a spring.

God's love is simply unlike anything we will ever comprehend. We can run as far away from God as we want and he will be waiting for our return, always. We can choose other things over him repeatedly and he will still choose us, always. We can forget him, but he will not forget us. If we have been chasing other things, we can come back home today; his love is waiting.

Lord, forgive me for preferring other things over you. I give value to meaningless activities instead of giving it to time spent with you. Help me recognize when I am loving something more than I love you. Help me repent quickly.

STRUGGLING TO STEADY

Establish my footsteps in your word,
and do not let any wrongdoing have power over me.
PSALM 119:133 NASB

In case we are ever tempted to think that God uses only perfect people for his work, he made sure to bust that myth. A quick read through Scripture and we see just how flawed God's people were: Moses murdered a man in his anger, David committed adultery, Peter denied ever knowing Jesus, and Paul persecuted believers before coming to Christ.

The Psalms are full of cries to God. Those who wrote the Psalms plead to the Lord that they are kept steadily on the path of righteousness, putting sin aside. If you are struggling with sin in your life, do not believe the lie that you cannot be used by God. Pray instead, as the psalmist did, that God will keep your steps steady, so you are always growing in faithfulness toward God. Whether you are a mom who yells, a friend who envies, or an employee who is dishonest, bask in the mercy of God who takes broken, struggling people and redeems them for his glory.

Thank you, Lord, for using a broken, struggling person like me for your purposes. Thank you for not requiring perfection. Thank you for not giving up on making me holy. I am humbled by your mercy!

ON THE WINNING TEAM

"Because he has loved me, I will save him;
I will set him securely on high,
because he has known my name."
PSALM 91:14 NASB

Sometimes we forget that loving the Lord comes with many advantages. The world often makes Christians feel like the weirdos, the outcasts, the ones who choose to skip the good things in life. But really, we are the ones who are winning! Because we love God, we have promise upon promise of good things. Not everything is in this lifetime, but this lifetime is not all there is.

Because we love God, we are part of a family that is not bound by blood or lineage. Because we love God, we have security which no amount of money, weapons, or provisions can ever provide. Because we love God, we are untouchable by our enemies even if they kill us. Because we love God, we live within the realm of mercy and the sovereignty of a good God. Because we love God, we can live with injustice, knowing that our enemies will be defeated in the end. Because we love God, we are saved.

Lord, forgive me for ever believing that by following you I am missing out on something. You give such good gifts to those who love you. May I never take them for granted, and may I continue to love you with all of my heart.

NIGHTTIME PROMISES

I stay awake all night
so I can think about your promises.
PSALM 119:148 NCV

We've surely all had our sleepless nights. Whether we had a coffee too late in the day, there's a newborn in the house who thinks it's time to party, or our anxious thoughts won't turn off, sleep evades all of us at some point. Watching the hours tick by causes so much anxiety in anticipation of a tired tomorrow.

The psalmist lacked sleep too, but instead of letting his mind wander into worry or become overwhelmed with exhaustion, he chose to meditate on the promises of God throughout his night. What might that do for us? It might cause us to remember that God is the one in control, not us. It might cause us to be thankful that not every night is a sleepless one. It might cause us to worship the God who created day and night, work and rest, and the promise of eternity where the lack of sleep will never bother us again. Next time we find ourselves tossing and turning, let's turn our thoughts to the promises of God.

God, thank you for creating our bodies to need rest. Forgive me for allowing anxiety to rule my sleepless nighttime moments. Help me steady my thoughts on you and allow your peace to rule my heart.

GOOD PLANS

Many are the plans in the mind of a man,
but it is the purpose of the LORD that will stand.
PROVERBS 19:21 ESV

Maria woke up with a plan. There was a lot to be done, and nothing would stand in the way of her agenda. She would not tolerate unruly kids, chatty neighbors, road closures, or out of stock items. She was going to make things happen! Only it turned out that God had other plans. Repeatedly throughout the day, the items on Maria's agenda just could not be fulfilled. Her frustration built until finally the Spirit brought this verse from Proverbs to mind: "Many are the plans in the mind of a man, but it is the purpose of the Lord that will stand."

God will ensure that his plan is in place even if it completely goes against ours. But on the days when our plans are upended, we must remember that his plan is better than ours. His plan leads us on straighter paths than we can ever make for ourselves. Today we submit our agendas to the Lord. We invite him to wreck them if it means that his way is fulfilled!

God, let me loosen the commitment to my plans enough that I can see the purpose of yours. I know you will have your way, so teach me to be willing to submit to your good and perfect plan.

READY FOR BATTLE

Be strong in the LORD and in his mighty power.
EPHESIANS 6:10 NLT

The lies of the enemy are pervasive in our world today.
Without a proper understanding of the truth, we can
quickly become overwhelmed by his tactics and fall for his
deceptions. What a relief, then, to know that God has given
us all we need to stand strong in the truth through the
reading of his Word and the presence of the Holy Spirit.

Acknowledging the spiritual battle is the first step and
recognizing our dependence on God is the second. Paul
wrote to the church in Ephesus that it is not by our might,
determination, or anything of our doing that causes us to
remain steadfast in our fight against the enemy. It is by
the strength of God and what he supplies that makes us
strong. The truth of his Word, righteousness, peace, faith,
and the empowerment of the Spirit is where we find our
strength. We can clothe ourselves with these things and
pray for discernment. Then we will be able to distinguish
the good and the evil in the spiritual battles we face daily.

Thank you, God, that you did not leave me to fight my
battles on my own. You have supplied all I need to defeat
the enemy. Help me be aware of Satan's tactics so I can
remain steadfast in my fight.

KEEPING UP APPEARANCES

The LORD said to Samuel, "Do not consider his appearance
or his height, for I have rejected him. The LORD does not
look at the things people look at. People look at the
outward appearance, but the LORD looks at the heart."

1 SAMUEL 16:7 NIV

How many hours have we spent making ourselves look
acceptable to our society? The world tells us that we need
to have laundry done, gray hairs hidden, homes cleaned,
and kids kept out of the mud. Keeping up appearances is
a full-time job designed by the devil to prevent us from
keeping up our hearts.

But God does not value the things the world values.
He would rather we focus on our relationships with
others than on what we are wearing. He would rather
we forgive the sins of our wrongful neighbor than fight
the injustice in court. He would rather we put time into
developing our characters instead of our appearances. We
need to consider the ways that we are making ourselves
acceptable to the world but failing to keep our hearts
right before the Lord. What should we change today?

Lord, forgive me for putting my focus on my outward
appearance and that of my home, rather than on the state
of my heart. Help me know how to wisely use my time,
what to invest my energy into, and how to please and
glorify you.

WINNING

Put on then, as God's chosen ones, holy and beloved, compassionate hearts, kindness, humility, meekness, and patience, bearing with one another and, if one has a complaint against another, forgiving each other; as the LORD has forgiven you, so you also must forgive. And above all these put on love, which binds everything together in perfect harmony.

COLOSSIANS 3:12-14 ESV

"I win!" you shout triumphantly. Whether you are in a disagreement with your sibling or proving yourself right to a friend, it's easy to place great value on being right and having things go the way you want. But true winning is not when everything goes the way you want it to.

You are a true winner when you respond to your friend or your circumstances in the way that Jesus would want you to respond. It's anticipating that God's goodness and grace will look different than your natural mindset. It's keeping quiet in a disagreement even when you know you're right because you value the relationship more than winning the fight. What might winning look like today?

God, help me value the things that you value by loving my neighbor more than I love being right. Teach me to respond in kindness and humility when someone wrongs me.

A WILLING STUDENT

The teaching of your word gives light,
so even the simple can understand.
PSALM 119:130 NLT

In college Janie was astounded by the critical thinking
required by her professors. Nothing in life prepared
her to analyze a text and write essays the way that was
now expected. Her mind couldn't wrap itself around the
abstract illustrations that supposedly held great depth
and meaning. She felt useless in class discussions.

We have all likely experienced this frustration or
confusion in different situations. It can leave us feeling
overwhelmed, useless, and ineffective. Thankfully, the
Christian life doesn't require us to have all the answers
in order to be used by God. All that is needed is a willing
heart which is steeped in the Word. Psalm 119 says that
God's Word brings insight, light, and revelation to those of
us who study and read with our minds and hearts open to
the conviction of the Holy Spirit.

God, thank you for your Word which gives me insight as I
meditate on it. May I always be led by your Spirit so I can
grow in the knowledge of you. My heart is willing. Please
use me, Lord.

NOVEMBER

"Salt is good, but if
the salt loses its salty taste,
you cannot make it salty again.
So, be full of salt,
and have peace with
each other."

MARK 9:50 NCV

EYES ON THE GOAL

My comfort in my suffering is this:
your promise preserves my life.
PSALM 119:50 NIV

Scripture is full of the stories of suffering saints. In Hebrews 11:35-38, we read the details of some of those who loved Jesus enough to suffer for him through horrific circumstances, knowing that he is a good God with good plans. In James 5 we read about the prophets who suffered significantly as they spoke the words given to them by God. How did they remain faithful to the call under such persecution? They had the end in sight, which was based on hope in God's promise of eternity.

When we look at our present challenges, we feel overwhelmed and defeated. But if we, like the prophets, are able to keep our eyes on the goal, we can live through anything. Whether we are facing persecution, challenges in our families, misunderstandings at work, or infertility or loss, we need to turn our eyes upon the promise of the eternal joy to come.

God, I know that you allow your loved ones to suffer, but I also know that I can trust your plan. Your people have been setting their eyes on you for millennia in order to press through trials. I can, too. Help me remain steadfast in you!

SELF OR SACRIFICE

We pursue the things which make for peace
and the building up of one another.
ROMANS 14:19 NASB

"You do you," is a phrase we often hear these days, and perhaps you've even said it yourself. It is one more nod toward the reign of individuality that permeates our culture. It puts the focus on what is best according to one person rather than what is best according to God. It causes us to think less about the sacrifices we can make on behalf of other people. Instead, it centers our focus on pleasing ourselves.

Are we exalting self-centeredness in our you-do-you-and-I'll-do-me society? What if we said to ourselves, "What would God have me do in this situation?" Sure, it doesn't slip off the tongue as easily, but it allows us to consider how to benefit others and bless the Lord. Jesus was the ultimate example of self-sacrifice. Let's see Jesus as our example!

Lord, it is sometimes easier to accept the cultural norms than to consider what a better alternative might be. Everything you did was ultimately because of your love of people. I want my life to reflect that too. Help me do what is best for others and will glorify you.

THANKFULNESS

Give thanks to the LORD, for he is good.
His love endures forever.
PSALM 136:1 NIV

November is known to many as a month to give thanks. We spend extra time this month considering the good things in our lives and thanking God for his blessings. Of course, we know that thankfulness is not limited to this one month of the year, and if we practice it already, then we know the joy and contentment that it brings.

Psalm 136 is the perfect template to follow in order to acknowledge what the Lord has done and to praise him for his faithfulness. If we struggle to find gratitude or we are in a heavy mood, we can apply today's psalm to our lives in order to recognize God's goodness again. We start by naming his attributes, speaking about the mighty things he has done, and acknowledging the ways he has shown his love. His love endures forever; may our praises follow suit!

Thank you, God, for your faithfulness to your people for thousands of generations. May I not dwell in a mindset of thankfulness this month only, but every day of the year. You are so good and worthy of my praise at every moment.

ANTICIPATING GOOD TODAY

Commit your way to the LORD;
trust in him, and he will act.
PSALM 37:5 ESV

Anticipation of the good things in eternity can supply motivation and determination through a difficult season when we are weary. But what happens when we anticipate the good things in life to come and drag our feet through the less-than-magnificent moments of this lifetime?

Certainly, our hope is built on the promise of eternity, but when we allow ourselves to focus only on the good that we foresee coming in that life then we miss all the good that God wants to give us right now. We can miss the beauty in the hard, messy seasons. We can ask the Holy Spirit to change our mindsets so we anticipate what he will do today in our normal and sometimes difficult lives. We will miss so much if we only wait for the best of times later.

Lord, I know that you have good for me right here, right now. Help me to not get so caught up in what I hope will come that I miss the gifts you are giving me today.

No Record of Wrongs

LORD, if you kept a record of our sins,
who, O LORD, could ever survive?
But you offer forgiveness,
that we might learn to fear you.
PSALM 130:3-4 NLT

Can you imagine if God kept a running record of our
mistakes? "Yikes, she yelled at her kids again… that's the
fourth time today." Or perhaps, "Wow, that makes eleven
cases of gossip this month." It sounds a bit absurd to
consider, but that is only because we know that God's
attention toward us is not consumed with recording our
mistakes; there would be little time left for anything else if
he did!

No, we who are cleansed by the blood of Christ do not
need to fear a long list of our wrong doings. It is his
forgiveness that defines our lives after salvation. What a
sweet reality that we face as God's children. In our own
lives and with those near to us, do we keep any record of
offenses, even if just in our minds? We need to strive to
offer the same forgiveness that God extends to us daily.

Lord, I know that without your forgiveness I could never
stand in your presence. And yet you have once and for all
extended mercy when I deserved punishment. Oh God,
teach me to do the same for people in my own life.

Increased Strength

On the day I called, you answered me;
You made me bold with strength in my soul.
PSALM 138:3 NASB

Some days drain everything out of us. We give all we can, physically, emotionally, and even spiritually. On the days when we are "running on fumes," we need to call to the Lord; repeatedly throughout all time he has met his people in their distress and given them what they needed in the moment they need it.

Psalm 138 says that when we call on God, he increases strength within us. What might it look like for us to be strengthened today? Do we need strength to push through a grueling day of work with enough grace to be kind to our coworkers? Do we need strength to be a listening ear to someone who is struggling, even when we are already emotionally worn out? Do we need strength to respond with gentleness to our husband or children when they are aggravating? We simply need to ask the Holy Spirit for the strength we need today, and he will supply it!

God, I am so thankful that you did not leave me to make it through each day on my own. When I am feeling worn out, please strengthen me to do what you have called me to do with the gentleness, patience, and kindness that only you can give.

PRECIOUS

How precious are your thoughts about me, O God.
They cannot be numbered!
I can't even count them;
they outnumber the grains of sand!
And when I wake up,
you are still with me!
PSALM 139:17-18 NLT

What a special statement! God's thoughts toward us are precious. We wonder what people think about us, don't we? As we shop, as we interact with our children in public places, as we work and attend church, we wonder how we are perceived, and we hope that we are seen in a good light.

What a gift it is, then, that we do not need to wonder how God perceives us. We are told in Psalm 139 that his thoughts toward us are precious and innumerable. God doesn't have just one or two good thoughts about each of us; they are countless! We can rest in the confidence of knowing that the God who made each of us regards us as precious.

It is comforting, God, to know that I do not need to wonder what you think about me. Even on my worst days you regard me as worthy of love and flawless. Help me pay more attention to your thoughts of me than the thoughts of others. I want to walk in confidence today as someone who knows she is loved.

SHELTER

I cried out to you, O LORD:
I said, "You are my refuge,
my portion in the land of the living."
PSALM 142:5 NKJV

"I checked the radar, and the storm won't hit us," Tasha said confidently to her nervous daughter. But five minutes later the whole family was huddled in the basement while tornado sirens wailed, and rain and wind violently lashed the house. Sometimes we have no time to prepare for the storms that hit, but where we take shelter makes all the difference for the outcome.

Do you shelter in your job? Are you putting all your mental energy into work to distract yourself from reality? Do you shelter in televisions shows? Are you drowning out your own life while investing emotional energy into the artificial lives of others? Do you shelter in the apps on your phone? Are you zoning out because the stress in real life is too hard? When we shelter in these things we might find temporary satisfaction, but there will be disappointment when a real event or issue brings us back to reality. Shelter instead in Christ. He is your good portion here, now, in the midst of every trial or storm.

Lord, when I am sheltering in a false hope, call me back to the reality that you are my true shelter and the only One who will ever satisfy my heart.

WORTHY OF GRACE

Israel, wait for the LORD;
for with the LORD there is mercy,
and with him is abundant redemption.
PSALM 130:7 NASB

Grace sometimes irks us, doesn't it? It irks us because we want it to go to people whom we think have earned it. Some people do not deserve grace according to our standards, and yet the Lord is gracious to them anyway; it's upsetting! What about those of us who have worked hard to be worthy of God's good gifts, especially his love and his compassion?

But isn't that the thing about grace—it is always undeserved. It is always given according to the gracious giver and not according to what someone has done or not done. It's not up to us to choose who God loves and who he decides to favor. God will give abundant redemption to the one he has chosen. We can be more in the character of God if we search our hearts for anyone we might be withholding grace from and give as Jesus would give. We can ask the Lord to reveal our own need for grace so we can learn to extend it to others.

Holy Spirit, help me understand my desperate need for grace. I do not want to be one who has followed all the rules outwardly but is hiding this offense against someone else. Forgive me and teach me to be gracious!

NO NEED TO IMPRESS

He takes no pleasure in the strength of a horse
or in human might.
No, the LORD's delight is in those who fear him,
those who put their hope in his unfailing love.
PSALM 147:10-11 NLT

All of our best efforts are not impressive to God. He isn't impressed by our strength, our independence, our talents, our level of responsibility, or our hard work. We can have the most successful day in our own minds but have totally missed the mark according to God. Why? Because God values our hope in his unfailing love and our worship of him as God alone.

Do our lives reflect an understanding and a belief that God is not at all impressed by all the things we do? He doesn't need a perfect resume, a spotless home, well-raised children, or several Ironman races. More than anything he wants a heart that is dedicated to his ways, a willingness to sacrifice the approval of others, and the humility to live a life dependent on him.

Lord, help me believe the truth that you are most pleased by a heart that is captivated by you alone. May all these other things fall to their proper places when hope in your unfailing love is the most important thing in my life.

IN ALL THINGS

He is before all things,
and in him all things hold together.
COLOSSIANS 1:17 NIV

There is beauty in realizing that life as we know it is because of Jesus Christ. Our days exist because Jesus made them possible initially and make them possible day after day. He is deeply connected to all we say and do, and no part of our lives is unseen, hidden, or forgotten by him. He is there in the wakeful night when we hoped for sleep, in the piles of laundry, in the shuttling of kids to after-school activities, in the meal-making and the walk-taking. He's present in the worries, the pressures, the love, and the concerns that fill up our hearts and minds. He knows all of it.

If we feel lost in the hustle of daily life, or if we're lonely and without a friend, or if we're simply too tired, we know that we aren't living life on our own. God is deeply involved in every single aspect of our lives. We can talk to him about any of it. We can pray, cry, yell, or sing. He is so happy to interact with us in this life which he has given us.

Thank you, Jesus, for being present with me in every part of my life. Help me believe that you are with me. Help me see the ways that you are before all things and hold all things together.

MORE TO LEARN

Who has known the mind of the LORD,
or who became his counselor?
ROMANS 11:34 NASB

We will never come to the end of learning new things
about God. There is always something new to discover.
We learn from the Scriptures, from the body of Christ, and
as revealed by the Holy Spirit. If we ever feel that we have
God figured out, we simply need to ask the Spirit to burst
open the boxes which we have placed him in, even if we
have done so unknowingly. We should pray that God will
refresh us with a new perspective and show us something
that we have missed before.

Today, we can challenge ourselves to read a passage of
Scripture which we have read previously. But this time we
need to read it with the intention of finding something
that we hadn't noticed before; we should search for
something about God's character, about what he does, or
about his interactions with mankind. Then we can ask the
Spirit to guide us in continuing to reveal new things; his
living and active Word will not disappoint us.

God, forgive me for ever thinking that I have come to the
end of learning about you. Your ways are so much higher
than mine, and there is always something new to learn!

CROWNED

He redeems me from death
and crowns me with love and tender mercies.
PSALM 103:4 NLT

Remember in the fairy tale stories how a man is knighted or a maiden is crowned queen? It is always done when the knight or maiden has been found worthy of honor. Never does a crown just fall from the sky, and never does a man trip over the sword with which he is knighted. Instead, there is a proper ceremony in the presence of others.

Now with that in mind, read today's verse from today's psalm— "He redeems me from death and crowns me with love and tender mercies." The love and mercy of God do not just happen to find you. They do not fall from the sky and magically just fall upon you with no explanation. They are intentional and thoughtful. They are a crown upon your head because God has found you worthy of honor. Wear your crown with confidence, sister. It is a blessing and an honor to be chosen by the Lord.

Thank you, God, for seeing me as worthy of your love and mercy. Help me receive it and to walk in love and mercy toward others today.

WORDS

I will sing to the LORD all my life;
I will sing praise to my God as long as I live.
May my meditation be pleasing to him,
as I rejoice in the LORD.
PSALM 104:33-34 NIV

What attitude do your words most reflect? Does praise flow from your heart with words demonstrating thankfulness, contentment, and grace? Or do your words tend to reflect a heart that is discontent? Do you complain or gossip? Do you tear down those around you with your speech rather than build them up?

If your heart is focused on pouring out praise, you will find it increasingly difficult to use your words for anything that will not bring glory to God. Today, think about the way you talk. Examine yourself to see if your words reflect a heart that is content in the Lord. If you find yourself complaining or using your words to hurt others, ask the Spirit to bring conviction and change.

God, I know I do not always use my words in ways that please you. Forgive me. Please give me a heart that is sensitive to your Spirit so that I can be aware of the times that I am not bringing glory to you.

GRACE INSTEAD

He will not constantly accuse us,
nor remain angry forever.
PSALM 103:9 NLT

Have you ever been accused of wrongdoing by someone who refused to hear the truth of your innocence? Or perhaps you did do something wrong to someone and then apologized, but forgiveness was refused? Pent up, harbored anger is destructive in relationships and leaves no room for growth. While we may experience it in our relationships with others, it is such a comfort to know that we do not have to live with the anger of God even though we have all deserved his wrath.

Our relationships with God may be the only relationship in our lives in which we receive complete forgiveness when we deserve anger and resentment. What then, should our responses be? As Paul said in Romans 6, we are, "by no means!" to keep on sinning so that grace may abound to us; instead, our lives are dedicated to the Lord and righteous living because we understand what punishment we deserve and yet what grace we live with. Praise the Lord!

Thank you, God, for the grace that abounds to me even when I deserve your anger. May your mercy keep me humble and may I respond with a life dedicated to pursuing righteousness.

FOCUS

May the words of my mouth
and the meditation of my heart
be acceptable in your sight,
LORD, my rock and my Redeemer.
PSALM 19:14 NASB

Is your mind wandering today? Focus is hard to come
by these days. The news causes anxiety, our jobs carry
stress into our homes, and our children pepper us with
curious questions; all of it combines to cause our minds to
jump from one thing to another, and we end up lacking
direction for our days or for our hearts. Consider the things
that may be causing your mind to wander; there may be
stress in your workplace or your home life; you may be
on your phone in every spare moment; or maybe you are
lacking any goals for the day.

Now steady your heart on the things that will cause your
mind to focus on what really matters: you have been bought
by the blood of Jesus and are a slave to righteousness; you
have been called and equipped for the task at hand; you
have the hope of eternity with Jesus. Ground yourself upon
these truths and pray for grace to focus your mind on things
that will please the Lord!

God, help me see what I can let go of to be able to better
focus on truth and things that will propel me into a deeper
understanding of you.

SHOWING LOVE

"A new commandment I give to you,
that you love one another: just as I have loved you,
you also are to love one another."
JOHN 13:34 ESV

What is the last thing someone did for you that made you feel loved? Chances are it wasn't some extravagant gesture with a flash mob and five-star restaurant. Perhaps it was a note from a friend, a task completed without being asked by your child or husband, or a compliment on a day you didn't feel beautiful.

When Jesus gave us the command to love one another, he wasn't expecting extravagance. Instead, he wanted us to use what we have in our hands and hearts. It may be the smallest gesture, but it can truly bless someone. Do not get caught up in believing that you must do something perfectly or very grand to show love. Don't think that you can't have any struggles before you reach out to someone else. What is in your hand today? What small thing can you do to demonstrate the love of Jesus? Offer it into the life of someone and watch Jesus multiply it like the loaves and fishes.

God, sometimes I feel unworthy of showing love when I am struggling myself but help me to remember that you do not require perfection. May I take every opportunity to show love just as you do for me.

PATIENCE

I waited patiently for the LORD;
he turned to me and heard my cry.
PSALM 40:1 NIV

We are all pretty good at demanding patience from others, but not necessarily good at practicing it ourselves. When we are struggling, we beg the Lord to save us, and to free us from the struggle. And what happens if he doesn't answer immediately? Our faith can dwindle, and we look for ways to solve the problem ourselves.

But what if we could learn, as David wrote in Psalm 40, to wait patiently for the Lord? What if we could ask for relief and then thank God for the trial, all in the same breath? Maybe we are waiting for something in our lives today. Maybe we have been struggling year after year, wondering when God will answer our prayers. We can be assured that he hears our cries. He knows our struggles, and he knows the good that will come from us waiting through them. We can ask the Lord for patience today and thank him for doing only what is good, including the wait.

Lord, I tend to think that I know what is best for me, but really, you do. Help me be patient, even in the time I am suffering, knowing that you are doing far more than I could ever comprehend.

POWERFUL

This was so they would keep his orders
and obey his teachings.
Praise the LORD!
PSALM 105:45 NCV

If you ever need a reminder of the sovereign power of God, read through Psalm 105. It is a summary of the history of Israel from the covenant God first made with Abraham, through the time he freed of Israelites from slavery, and then as he brought them into the Promised Land four decades later. Again and again, we are reminded of the power of God to save his people, to strike down those who work against him, and to guide and guard his chosen ones. And what was the purpose of all these amazing acts? That his people would respect his commands and obey him with reverential awe.

Can you make your own list of the powerful things the Lord has done to show himself faithful and worthy of your obedience? It might not include the parting of a sea or water gushing from the rocks in the desert, but the God we serve today is the same powerful God who rescued his people thousands of years ago. Consider now the ways God has shown himself worthy of your reverence.

Lord, your power has covered my life faithfully. Let me never take for granted the ways you showed yourself sovereign and faithful.

GROWTH IN DORMANCY

"Yes, I am the vine; you are the branches. Those who
remain in me, and I in them, will produce much fruit.
For apart from me you can do nothing."
JOHN 15:5 NLT

As fall makes way for winter, the signs of life all around
are going dormant. Bare trees, brown grasses, and the
fruit stripped from the summer gardens all remind us that
the natural world takes a season of rest through the cold
season, waiting for the growth that will happen when
warmth and sun return.

Dormancy may happen in the natural world, but it does not
need to happen in our souls. Life's winters do not need to
cause us to hibernate from challenges or opportunities to
grow. Times of rest and respite are good times to allow new
things to emerge. We do not need to hide away waiting for
spring before we grow. We can pursue whatever God what
he has planned for us even during the dormant months. He
has plans for our souls in this winter season.

Lord, let me not hide away during challenging seasons.
When life all around me has gone into rest, I open my
heart to what you have planned for me.

DWELLING ON TRUTH

"You shall know the truth,
and the truth shall make you free."
JOHN 8:32 NKJV

What does our self-talk sound like most often? Our thoughts are powerful in influencing the way we think about ourselves. We quickly begin to believe the thoughts that we tend to dwell on, which is why knowing and meditating on the truth of God's Word is so important. Simple thoughts like, "I'm not cut out for this," or "I can't do this; it's too hard," are just the first step to spiraling into a pattern of defeated and destructive thinking.

This will inevitably lead us into walking through our days with a negative attitude in all aspects of life. We desperately need to fill our minds with thoughts based on the truth of the Word to counter this destructive thinking. We should live and walk in godliness, not just live and get by. We are not subject to sin, bad attitudes, or selfishness. We have the power of the Spirit enabling us to live well today. May truth guard our hearts and minds in Christ Jesus today!

God, thank you for the truth that sets me free. Your Word brings life, not condemnation. Fill me with your truth and help me recognize patterns of destructive thinking so I can remain grounded in you throughout my day.

LOVED TO LOVE

We love because he first loved us.
1 JOHN 4:19 NIV

Sometimes the kind of love we demand from others does not make mistakes, does not falter, and always does as we wish. But if that were the kind of love that God demanded from us, we would never have received it! God did not wait for us to obey before first loving us. His love does not give up on us or draw a line and say, "You've messed up too many times." His love does not reprimand in anger. It is patient and kind, full of grace and always pursuing us.

What kind of love are you extending to the people in your life? Does your love give grace upon grace, or is it easily revoked? Does your love continually pursue, or does it give the silent treatment? Does your love wait patiently, even in suffering, or is it abandoned at the first sign of contention or disagreement? Remember the love with which your Savior has loved you. Pray for that same love to flow from you to the people around you.

Jesus, you have loved me so that I can love others. Your love is humble, patient, and kind. Please help me remember your love throughout my day, and to love in the same way.

BLESSINGS

Blessed be the God and Father of our LORD Jesus Christ, who has blessed us with every spiritual blessing in the heavenly places in Christ.

EPHESIANS 1:3 NASB

The blessings of God are hidden throughout our days, but we only notice his many gifts when we are conscious and looking for them. Different things may be preventing us from seeing, hearing, or receiving his blessings today. We can be distracted from noticing God in our lives by exhaustion, sickness, or conflict. Distractions can turn our thoughts so far inward that we miss the blessings that God is holding out to us.

Regardless of our circumstances today, we can ask God to keep our eyes open, our ears attentive, and our hearts soft to the things he wants to speak to us. We can be determined to notice the goodness that he is offering us. If we start our days by setting our minds on the truth, then ask the Holy Spirit to keep us focused, then we won't be letting Satan steal the blessings that God is giving us.

Lord, may I not be near-sighted today, seeing only the challenges that arise and the troubles that pursue me. May I look outward, noticing the goodness you have for me and the opportunities I have to love others as you have loved me.

No Bows or Swords

I do not trust in my bow;
I do not count on my sword to save me.
You are the one who gives us victory over our enemies;
you disgrace those who hate us.
O God, we give glory to you all day long
and constantly praise YOUR name.
PSALM 44:6-8 NLT

What should we be trusting in to bring victory to our lives? Do we tend to rest on our talents, wealth, intelligence, determination, or resilience? We do naturally turn to our strengths to bring us out in victory, but the reality is that even the strongest characteristics will fall short of rescuing us. So where is our hope? The Lord can always be trusted to bring us to victory.

Whatever you face today, whatever battle you are fighting or sin you are struggling with, do not put your trust in your "bow" or "sword." They will fail you, but the Lord will not. Cry out to him in your struggles. Depend on his strength to free you and sustain you. Admit to him your inability to handle the situation even with your strongest capabilities. He will come through for you.

God, I quickly turn to my own talents to get me through, but I know that I will fail again and again. Help me remember that even my greatest skills will not see me through to victory.

RECIPIENTS OF MERCY

Once you were not a people, but now you are the people
of God; once you had not received mercy, but now you
have received mercy.

1 PETER 2:10 NIV

Once upon a time, we were nobodies. We were trapped in
sin, condemned to death, and hopeless to save ourselves.
Then God in his mercy chose us to be part of his family.
We went from being unrecognizable to being God's own
possession chosen and sought after. We are the people
picked to praise him and recipients of his mercy.

Our lives should be lived in response to this great truth
with less complaining and more thankfulness. We should
have less, "I want" and more, "what is your will?" We should
live less in pursuit of the created and more in pursuit of
the Creator. He who deemed us as worthy to bear his
image and reflect his glory has made us his people. Do
we live in a way that shows we believe this to be our true
identity? We praise him for his mercy today.

Thank you, God, that in your goodness you chose me to
receive your mercy. You took someone deserving of death
and gave me life. May I live my life in response to that
mercy by giving thanks, praising you, and telling of your
goodness to those I meet.

GIFT OF COMMUNITY

Let us not neglect our meeting together, as some people do, but encourage one another, especially now that the day of his return is drawing near.

HEBREWS 10:25 NLT

In today's society, our lives are often buried under mountains of work. It often consumes our time, our mental energy and clarity, and our emotional well-being. In addition, we can end up isolated because we simply don't have the time or capacity to connect with others. But God created us to live in community, especially with other believers.

When our lives become so consumed by our work that we don't have opportunities to be with other people who love Jesus, our relationship with the Lord suffers. We face burnout much quicker when we're overworked. But when we interact with believers, we are blessed by their company and their encouragement. We come away from our shared time filled and ready to make it through whatever lies ahead. If we have neglected community with the body of Christ, we should plan right now to initiate time with a friend or a group of friends. We need that time to get together to encourage one another.

Lord, I know that the family of God is a gift! Let me not become so busy with the rest of my life that I fail to take part in the community that you created for me to live in.

GRACE AND GOODNESS

May the favor of the LORD our God rest on us;
establish the work of our hands for us—
yes, establish the work of our hands.

PSALM 90:17 NIV

What should we be looking for in life today? We tend to live for things that make us feel good or that please us and fulfill our desires. But what if we went into our days looking for evidence of God's grace and goodness? What if, instead of setting our hearts on success or getting what we want, we set our hearts on seeing all the indications of God's faithfulness that we can find?

If we pray today for eyes to see just that, then we might notice little instances of glory. We might see God's goodness in getting us safely to work. We would praise him for providing for an unforeseen car expense. We can thank him for the beautiful morning to spend with our children. Those aren't coincidences and they aren't karma. That is God being gracious and loving and taking good care of each of us, his children.

God, you surround me with favor like a shield. Thank you for the evidence of your goodness and faithfulness which fills every moment of my day. Give me eyes to see your grace in my life. May I never neglect to praise you for it!

Purpose

The LORD will fulfill his purpose for me;
your steadfast love, O LORD, endures forever.
PSALM 138:8 ESV

Sometimes we get set on a course or direction in our lives. Then one day we wake up realizing that we're going through the motions of what we need to do without really knowing why we're doing it. That lack of purpose can cause us to feel that we aren't being useful to God. Then we question whether or not we are even doing what we're supposed to be doing. It is a defeating spiral.

While it is not wrong to want to feel God's purpose in our lives or to know that God is finding us useful, the desire for those feelings can't be our goal. Instead, our goal ought to be faithfulness to the task at hand. We need to keep our gaze focused on Jesus as our example of faithfulness. We can ask him daily what his will for us is, even moment by moment. Everything will make sense in the end, and our faithfulness will bless the One who sets our purpose in life to begin with.

Lord, I do want to know that I am being used by you but forgive me when I let that become a need of mine. You have asked me to remain faithful in walking in godliness. I can trust that you are using me in ways that I cannot see or imagine when I am doing what I know you have called me to do.

SET APART

Your eyes saw my unformed body;
all the days ordained for me were written in your book
before one of them came to be.
PSALM 139:16 NIV

Even when we don't understand the why of things in our lives, we can take comfort in knowing that God planned our days before a single one of them began. We were fearfully set apart (v.14) for his work before our lives came into existence. The Hebrew word used in verse fourteen is *palah* which means "to be distinct, marked out, be separated, distinguished, to be wonderful." Our lives, which are often full of things we do not understand, were penned by a God who set us apart for a distinct and specific time and calling.

Sometimes there are things in our lives which we do not understand. That's a good reason today to thank the Lord for authoring our stories before our lives even began. We can declare our trust in his good plan for our lives. We do not need to attempt to rewrite any part of our stories which God has already perfectly written.

Thank you, Lord, for setting me apart to be part of your plan for history. I am humbled that you chose me and wrote my story with perfect faithfulness.

TAKING BACK WHAT'S STOLEN

Be of sober spirit, be on the alert. Your adversary, the devil, prowls around like a roaring lion, seeking someone to devour. So resist him, firm in your faith, knowing that the same experiences of suffering are being accomplished by your brothers and sisters who are in the world.

1 PETER 5:8-9 NASB

It is healthy for the Christian to remember that we have an enemy who wishes to destroy us. Unlike the abundant life that Jesus desires for us, Satan will do all he can to tear us apart and cause us to doubt God's goodness.

We should take time to consider whether or not there is an area in our lives which can be identified as a target for Satan. It could be something that perhaps for years he has been bent on stealing from us. It could be a good relationship with a parent or sibling that he wants to send awry. We could be guilty of an incorrect view of ourselves. Possibly there's an addiction that has taken years of energy and focused living away from us. How might God want to restore this area and bring healing and an understanding of the truth?

God, I know that my enemy is real and eager to destroy me. Help me, by the power of your Spirit, to walk in awareness of my enemy, so I can fight for freedom.

DECEMBER

Lead me in your truth
and teach me,
For You are the God
of my salvation;
For You I wait all the day.

PSALM 25:5 NASB

MORE GRACE

God gives us even more grace.
JAMES 4:6 NCV

Just when you think you've come to the very end of God's desire to come through for you, he comes through again. Keep that in mind with whatever you face today or in your current season of life. Life right now, with its unique challenges, can be wonderful.

You serve a God who gives strength and grace afresh every single day. Ask him for the ability to choose hope amidst difficulty or amidst mundanities. Find the good that he gives you today. Rejoice and choose thankfulness regardless of your disappointments. Consider the attitude that you are reflecting to people in your life. Are you demonstrating hopefulness in a good and faithful God? Spend time now thanking him for the grace that never runs out. Find the specific ways that grace shows up in your life today.

God, I want my life to reflect my belief in your ability to supply all that I need for every single day. May I never lose faith in your ability to come through for me. May my words and behaviors demonstrate my hope in your faithfulness and goodness at all times.

REVERENCE

Israel, what does the LORD your God ask of you but to fear the LORD your God, to walk in obedience to him, to love him, to serve the LORD your God with all your heart and with all your soul, and to observe the LORD's commands and decrees that I am giving you today for your own good?
DEUTERONOMY 10:12-13 NIV

Reverence is not something we see much in today's culture. We disregard so much today because value has been stripped from most things that were revered in times past. This is seen in many ways from our acceptance of fast fashion and one-time-use items to our understanding of what it means to fear the Lord.

When we really revere God, it causes us to want to please him at all costs. Are there things in our lives which we are willing to forfeit in order to please God? We may be holding on to an item or a dream at the cost of holding God above it all. Do we believe so strongly in God's goodness and trustworthiness that we will sacrifice even the costliest possessions and desires as Abraham demonstrated? How can we show reverence for the Lord today?

God, I want my life to reflect that I deeply respect your Word and your commands, and that I love you with all that I am. Show me if there are areas of my life that I am holding back from you and help me to release them to you so I can walk in full surrender to your perfect ways.

THE GREATEST COMMANDS

"'Love the LORD your God with all your heart, all your soul, and all your mind.' This is the first and most important command. And the second command is like the first: 'Love your neighbor as you love yourself.'"

MATTHEW 22:37-39 NCV

Do you get distracted from the two greatest commandments: to love God with your all and to love others as you love yourself? Do you fill your mind and your heart with other things and forget that the Christian life comes down to these two commandments?

Pray today that you will be guided by the Spirit in your love. Pray for ears that hear every whisper of the Holy Spirit to reach out and listen to someone's voice. Pray for hands and feet that are quick to obey God's calling to serve someone in their need. Pray for eyes to see where love is needed the most. Pray for a creative mind that seeks to meet someone's silent cry. Pray that you will be sensitive to the Spirit, so you receive his guidance and walk according to his wisdom. Pray that you reflect his character at every moment. This is what he created you for!

Lord, I desire to love as you created me to love. Forgive me for being distracted from the two greatest commandments with so many insignificant things. Help me be sensitive to your leading so that I can love you and others well.

HEART-CHANGE

Come close to God and he will come close to you.
Cleanse your hands, you sinners;
and purify your hearts, you double-minded.
JAMES 4:8 NASB

Sin is primarily an internally sourced problem and not something caused by external circumstances. This is a hard pill to swallow because it forces us to face the source of our sin which is our hearts. We want to believe that our problems are caused by our spouse or our coworkers or even by the various troubles we face. But in reality, sin dwells within our hearts, and we will never overcome it by pointing fingers at the people or the happenings around us.

The wisdom in God's Word teaches us to deal with this internal issue. But really, how wonderful is it that we no longer need to follow a long list of dos and don'ts like the Israelites had to do under the old covenant? It is not up to us to save ourselves by perfecting our ability to follow instructions. We have grace which meets us continually in every new situation and after every fresh mistake. This grace saves, and this grace causes our hearts to respond to the merciful God who knew we could never save ourselves.

God, your grace continually humbles me. Thank you for seeing my sinful heart and providing a way for me to be cleansed. May I see my need for heart-change instead of blaming those around me for my sin.

CALLED TO BLESS

*"If you know these things,
blessed are you if you do them."*
JOHN 13:17 ESV

Life turns out differently when we let God orchestrate our days instead of pursuing selfish ambitions. "I don't feel like it," or "I'm too tired," are phrases we use too frequently as we excuse ourselves from those opportunities which the Lord intends as blessings. What if Jesus had said those things instead of healing the sick and preaching to thousands of people when really, he just wanted to be alone (Matthew 14)?

Who might the Lord be calling you to serve today even if you don't feel like it? How can you open yourself up to the possibility of being used by him, rather than locking your heart away where it feels safe but where it will actually decay? We were made for good works (Ephesians 2:10) and called to be a blessing to others (Genesis 12:2). If we choose to walk in willingness to the Spirit of God today, we will be witnesses to his blessings as we bless others.

Lord, I don't want to pursue selfishness and therefore miss opportunities to be useful to you in blessing others. Help me open my heart to service regardless of how I feel.

COUNTED

"Then you would guard my steps,
instead of watching for my sins."
JOB 14:16 NLT

We need to be reminded of this often: there is One who watches our every move, counts our steps, and guards us throughout our day. He also knows every single thing we do in secret, every word we speak that we shouldn't, and every evil or unkind thought. But in his mercy, he chooses to cover our disgraces and not keep track of them. He counts our steps, not our sins. He sees us as righteous, not sinful. He calls us beloved, not wretched.

Today, let's give praise to the one who could punish us for all the wrong we do but chooses instead to see us as precious and honored (Isaiah 43:4), new creations (2 Corinthians 5:17), and delightful (Zephaniah 3:17). We need to also remind ourselves to purposefully choose to see others in this way. We do not keep track of each other's wrongs against us or any of their many mistakes. We need to see them as covered in grace and worthy of love just as the Lord sees us.

Lord, thank you that while you see all, you only keep track of my steps and not my wrongdoings. I will never get over the grace that you daily pour out on me.

KNOWING GOD

"This is eternal life: that they know you, the only true God, and Jesus Christ, whom you have sent."

JOHN 17:3 NIV

Are you pursuing God like it's the most important thing you will ever do? Jesus came to earth with one goal in mind—to rescue sinners so they might know the one true God. How are we to know him if he is just one item on our long checklists for the day? Our lives are full, but they should never become so full that we neglect the one thing that our souls need.

Wherever we are in life, we can always remember this principle: Jesus brought us here to take us deeper. Whether that is in college, working hard at a challenging career, raising children at home, or retired, the goal of this life is to know God more. We should ask ourselves periodically if something is keeping us from making our relationship with Jesus the top priority above everything else. We need to be ruthless about removing from our lives anything that prevents us from going deeper with God.

Lord, reveal to me now anything that I have made more important than you. Remind me that the more I know you, the more I trust you. I want my life to be marked by pure trust because I have made knowing you the goal.

MANIFESTING CHRIST

We have troubles all around us, but we are not defeated.
We do not know what to do, but we do not give up the
hope of living. We are persecuted, but God does not leave
us. We are hurt sometimes, but we are not destroyed. We
carry the death of Jesus in our own bodies so that the life
of Jesus can also be seen in our bodies.

2 CORINTHIANS 4:8-10 NCV

We have been saved so that the life of Jesus can be
manifested through us. Do we consistently reflect joy in
our difficulties, thanksgiving in all circumstances, and
hope throughout troubled times? Do we seek to serve
instead of succumbing to being a victim? Are we beaten
down by life's challenges, allowing troubles and unfair
decisions to drive us to despair? Do we tend to pity
ourselves, causing us to freeze up or shrink back?

The Spirit of God lives within us, giving us the power to
overcome any issues we may face. Today, let's consider
whether we are acting out of the power of the Holy Spirit or
allowing fear, anxiety, or self-pity to rule our lives. We pray
that we will be strengthened by Christ on every occasion.

Lord, I want people to see Christ within me when they see
me. Forgive me for allowing anything but you to rule my
responses. Help me live today by the power of the Holy
Spirit.

THE RIGHT KIND OF REST

*"Come to me, all who are weary and burdened,
and I will give you rest."*

MATTHEW 11:28 NASB

"Come to me…and I will give you rest." We often cling to this promise when our lives have become overwhelmed with tasks. We've said yes too many times to too many church positions; we've taken on more than we can handle at work; our stress levels are through the roof. So, we come to Jesus for a break; he promises rest, right?

Yes, absolutely, he gives us rest. But it doesn't mean he will sing us to sleep. It means he will take our anxious thoughts about our many responsibilities and replace them with joy and vitality to do the work that *he* has called us to do. This may mean assessing priorities because it's not always good to indiscriminately do whatever we have deemed necessary for ourselves. God has to be in the believer's schedule. The Christmas season becomes busy for many of us. As we pray to Jesus, we can ask him what *he* has called us to. We need to ask him to give us the joy and strength for that schedule. Everything else can be set aside.

God, I want to be busy with the work you have called me to. I know that you will supply all my needs for the work that you have given me. Help me discern what can be set aside so that I can focus on what is important.

NOT THE GOAL

This is a trustworthy saying, and everyone should accept it: "Christ Jesus came into the world to save sinners"—and I am the worst of them all.
1 TIMOTHY 1:15 NLT

When it comes down to it, most of us can admit that we are spending our days looking for things to make us happy. We shop when we need a pick-me-up—retail therapy, anyone? We pour ourselves a glass of wine when the kids are in bed because we deserve it—any wine moms out there? Unfortunately, we carry this must-feel-good attitude over into our relationships with Jesus. Perhaps we don't actually ask Jesus how he will make us feel good, but the way we treat him reveals that this is what truly is in our hearts.

But Jesus didn't come as the Savior to make us feel better. He came to root out the things in our hearts and lives that will destroy us. Even though some things might look good like acceptance, success, or even material possessions, they can lead to death if we have them in our hearts with the wrong motivation. Even if Jesus' work in us can be painful for a time, it produces a result that is worth so much more than these temporary pleasures can ever produce.

Jesus, I am guilty of looking to you just so you can make things better in my life. Forgive me! You know what I need.

COMING RESTORATION

You number my wanderings;
Put my tears into your bottle;
Are they not in your book?
PSALM 56:8 NKJV

The "most wonderful time of the year" simply isn't
the most wonderful time for some people. Perhaps
Christmastime brings painful memories for you, or it's a
reminder of things you once had which have been lost.
Maybe you have good memories of family times together,
or loved ones who have passed away, or easier times in
life. If the Christmas season is hard for you, there are good
reasons for you not to feel burdened or sad.

Remember instead that this is the time when we celebrate
the life of One who came to restore all the sad things.
Jesus will give us joy instead of grief over all the things
that have been broken or lost. He came once, and he is
coming again. Not only that, but he knows your sorrow
now. He sees your broken heart and your story that brings
anguish to your soul. Pray for hope even in the pain
because restoration is coming.

God, thank you for knowing my pain and caring for every
part of me. I am encouraged to know that I am not alone.
Give me hope in the final restoration that you will bring.

STAY THE COURSE

Praise the LORD.
Blessed are those who fear the LORD,
who find great delight in his commands.
PSALM 112:1 NIV

Sometimes we awaken ready for the day and eager to face whatever comes at us. Other days we awaken moody and exhausted from too little sleep, only wanting to return to bed. On those days especially, we need to determinedly walk in righteousness within the power of the Holy Spirit.

We might even justify our behavior some days when we don't try to do what pleases God or stand up for what is right. Every day, whether it feels good or not, we need to set our eyes on the things of eternity instead of the temporal challenges that the day hands us. In Psalm 112 we read about the benefits of walking with God and doing what is good. It's not an exhaustive list of things that will happen to all believers, but it is a list of blessings that we can anticipate if we pursue righteousness even on our bad days. God's Word in Psalm 112 reminds us that no matter what happens today, he is worthy for us to stay the course.

God, when I am tired and grumpy, not in the mood to work at walking in righteousness, please remind me that it is always worth it to do what is right in your sight.

NEW PLANS

Depend on the LORD in whatever you do,
and your plans will succeed.
PROVERBS 16:3 NCV

It's usually this time of year when we start thinking about
what is coming next. A new year brings new goals, new
opportunities, and a chance to lay to rest that which
didn't go so well in the current year. Sometimes we use
the coming New Year as an excuse to stop trying now in
the last few days of this year, preferring to wait till January
for a fresh start. Sometimes we make so many plans and
goals that we overwhelm ourselves right from the start.
Sometimes we don't plan anything because we then can't
disappoint ourselves if we don't meet our goals.

Wherever we land in our planning for the New Year,
believers need to take all our plans, dreams, and desires
for the coming year to the Lord. We can talk through each
hope or aspiration and ask God, "Is this something you
want for me?" and "Will this goal benefit my walk with the
Lord and my relationships with those around me?" If you
commit your way to the Lord, *he* will act (Psalm 37:5). We
can't go wrong with that kind of planning.

Lord, as this year comes to a close, may I bring before you
all my plans and goals for the next year. I want to walk with
you, knowing that with you as my guide, I can't go wrong.

TO LOVE OTHERS

"You shall love the LORD your God with all your heart and with all your soul and with all your strength."
DEUTERONOMY 6:5 NASB

We will severely lack the things we need to live well alongside other people if we do not first cultivate a deep love for Jesus. In him, we will have patience, slowness to anger, and grace. We need to understand the ways of God before we will be able to impart his attributes and reflect them to others in our lives. How can we grow our love for God this week in our hearts and minds? How can we truly change our habits and our attitudes?

We can think of ways to push ourselves into a deeper love for the Lord. We might listen to Christian podcasts or an audio Bible while we are cooking or driving in the car. We can choose a passage of Scripture to memorize with the kids or our spouse. We might replace the time spent on the phone with time spent reading the Bible. Any time spent with God is never wasted or futile, and we will find in ourselves the graceful ability to extend love to others with the more time and effort we spend nurturing our love for the Lord.

Lord, if I am to love the people you put in my life, I know that first I need to love you well. Help me, God, to seek you continually, and to grow my love for those around me too.

DELIGHTED STUDY

His delight is in the law of the LORD,
and on his law he meditates day and night.
PSALM 1:2 ESV

How would you describe your reading times in the Word lately? Do you find yourself engaging in dutiful study or delighted study? Psalm 1 promises a rich blessing for the one who delights in the Lord's instruction: whatever he does prospers. The best way to have success in your life is to delight yourself in the instructions of the Lord.

What is holding you back from delighting in God's Word? Are you finding yourself distracted by other things? Are you giving yourself only a small window of time to study and read? Do you treat God's Word as something to be checked off the list, rather than something you do because you truly want to learn? The blessing of delighted study cannot be beaten by anything else. Ask the Lord to reveal what you need to surrender in order to get back to delighting in the Word.

God, I do not want my time in your Word to be something I do just because I think I have to, or because I've developed a habit of it without truly desiring it. Reveal to me the things I am making more important than delighting in your instructions so I can get back to a heart that truly loves you.

IN FAILURE AND SUCCESS

Of his fullness we have all received,
and grace upon grace.
JOHN 1:16 ESV

Shame mounts when we continually make the same mistakes or repeatedly struggle in the same area of life. We feel incapable of ever overcoming; Satan wants us to believe that we are trapped in our sin. But God's grace is present with us in both our failures and our successes, and we can access it at any moment.

Think about what it might look like to have a grace-based response to success in that area of struggle. It might be immediate thankfulness to God for meeting you and helping you to respond righteously. What about for failure? Accessing and responding to grace might mean you first repent, then thank God for his mercy. You can follow that by looking ahead to how you can do better next time, rather than dwelling on your shame or self-pity. Take hold of God's grace given specifically for you today.

Thank you, Lord, that your grace is available in my struggles and in my successes. Help me remember that I have access to your throne of grace at any time. I do not need to ever listen to Satan's lies!

RESPOND

The grace of God has appeared that offers salvation to all people. It teaches us to say "No" to ungodliness and worldly passions, and to live self-controlled, upright and godly lives in this present age, while we wait for the blessed hope—the appearing of the glory of our great God and Savior, Jesus Christ, who gave himself for us to redeem us from all wickedness and to purify for himself a people that are his very own, eager to do what is good.

TITUS 2:11-14 NIV

The day was off to a bad start before it even began. A strange pain kept Lena awake long into the night leaving her exhausted in the morning. Her kids woke up grouchy and argumentative. And Lena's emotions were all over the place thanks to hormones. She knew she had to make a choice for this day: allow her circumstances to dictate her mood or respond to Jesus' goodness in this less-than-ideal situation.

Everything that happens in our lives are Jesus' tools to draw us closer to him. The beautiful moments cause our hearts to respond in wonder and awe, and the challenging moments can cause us to respond to the faithfulness of his character. We have so many opportunities to lean into the character of Christ every day.

Lord, thank you that because you are good and trustworthy, I can respond to you with a thankful and humble heart. I can choose joy in each and every situation.

THE DAILY CHOICE

"If any of you wants to be my follower, you must give up your own way, take up your cross daily, and follow me."
LUKE 9:23 NLT

A lot of life entails choosing to do good when there is no immediate benefit or reward for us. Why would we choose this life of submission to God's ways, denying ourselves and taking up our crosses *daily*? The answer is one that doesn't go over well in our microwaveable, overnight-delivery culture. We find that obedience to God is one hundred percent worth it—eventually. This delayed gratification means that our fullness in Christ may not be tomorrow, next year, in ten years, or even within our lifetime. But with certainty we will find this glorious submission worth it when we arrive in eternity.

Every day we need to wake up and choose Jesus. We purposely choose to deny the old self that was put to death and put on the new self which is clothed in righteousness. Each day is a new opportunity to choose either Christ or the natural self. We pray that God will give his grace to help us carry our crosses today.

Lord, it is hard to walk faithfully when the reward seems far off. Give me the grace to choose you each new day, and to carry my cross with joy, knowing that it will be worth it in the end.

ANCHORED JOY

I will rejoice in the LORD;
I will take joy in the God of my salvation.
HABAKKUK 3:18 ESV

What have you anchored your joy upon lately? Is your joy rooted in the affirmation that others give you? Or do you only gain happiness when your children have success and happiness? Are your successes in your job or with your hobby the only true things that put you in your happy place? If your joy is anchored on anything but Christ, it will quickly fade with the changing seasons and the inevitability of imperfect circumstances.

Joy found in the Lord endures through pain, difficulty, and things not going your way. In Habakkuk 3:17-19, the prophet lists all the things that could have gone wrong for him: "Even though… and even though…" but instead of ending his prayer-song with a woe-is-me type of statement, he says, "Yet I will rejoice in the Lord, I will be joyful in God my Savior." What are your "even though" statements? Declare today that you will still rejoice in the Lord, your true source of complete and perfect joy.

God, even though things go wrong, and my days may not look the way I wanted them to, yet I will choose to rejoice in you. Thank you for giving me the opportunity day after day to choose to anchor my joy in Christ!

LOVING OUR ENEMIES

"You have heard that it was said, 'You shall love your neighbor and hate your enemy.' But I say to you, love your enemies, bless those who curse you, do good to those who hate you, and pray for those who spitefully use you and persecute you, that you may be sons of your Father in heaven."

MATTHEW 5:43-44 NKJV

Dana's seven-year-old came to her in tears. The neighborhood friends were playing happily with her, but soon they ran off to play by themselves leaving her alone and feeling unwanted. "Why are they so mean?" she demanded to know. Little girl drama can be hard to deal with, but Dana tried her best to find a way to instruct her daughter in how to manage her own hurt heart.

Truth be told, as adults we often still wonder why people are so mean, don't we? God doesn't promise perfect relationships, but he does give us wisdom in how to handle them. Love them. Pray for them. Whoever our enemies are today, we can ask the Holy Spirit to help us love them by praying for them and granting them the mercy that he first granted us.

God, it is so difficult to love those who do me wrong, but I can quickly forget that I was the one doing wrong to you when you extended love to me. Help me be merciful as you are merciful, and to love my enemies.

FAITHFUL DISCIPLINE

He is like a rock; what he does is perfect,
and he is always fair.
He is a faithful God who does no wrong,
who is right and fair.

DEUTERONOMY 32:4 NCV

God does no wrong. His faithfulness is constant, influencing every aspect of his character and our lives. Even his discipline is an act of faithfulness and an expression of love for us. It shows his deep care because he wants us to grow and have good things produced in our lives. His discipline brings holiness and peace to us; it is not to be shunned or opposed.

We need to take time today to consider how his perfect and just God's discipline has been. It has brought about the fruits of peace and righteousness in our lives. If there was ever a time when we were wandering, and his discipline brought us back, we have a powerful testimony to his faithful discipline. If we have pursued things which were not good for us, and he took them away to spare us heartache, we can speak about the heart of God. We can thank God today for the discipline he provides because from it we grow in wisdom.

Lord, while it is never pleasant at the time, thank you that you love me enough to discipline me. You want my heart, my righteousness, and my ultimate good.

THE GOAL

Though you have not seen him, you love him;
and even though you do not see him now,
you believe in him and are filled with an inexpressible
and glorious joy, for you are receiving the end result
of your faith, the salvation of your souls.

1 PETER 1:8-9 NIV

This whole Christianity thing is tough, but the end result
of this daily denial-of-self and the challenging life-of-
faith is written clearly for us in a way that motivates us to
keep pressing on. The goal that we are aiming for is the
salvation of our souls. Salvation is our goal. We don't shoot
for temporal happiness, success in our jobs, or a beautiful
home or family.

In our ever-changing world, the gift of salvation is one
constant that we can rely on. It will never be taken away
from us even when we struggle. It comes from God, and
we do not have to earn it by working hard. Once we have
come to God, he will never cast us away. We can forever
rest in the knowledge of God's good gift of salvation.

Lord, thank you for the gift of salvation. What a blessing
to know that it is not something I have to earn, and not
something that will be taken away even as I struggle. Help
me walk steadily toward your salvation. What a wonderful
goal I am aiming for!

PEACE

Christ himself is our peace.
EPHESIANS 2:14 NCV

Where do you look for peace in your life? It might be the approval of your husband, boss, or friends. You may find peace when everything goes according to plan in your day. Perhaps if you are a young mom, it is peaceful in the quietness during nap time or after the kids are in bed. But Paul told us in Ephesians that Christ himself is our peace. And Isaiah said that those who walk uprightly enter into peace (Isaiah 67:2).

In other words, our obedience to the Prince of Peace himself leads us into peaceful hearts. That is the only place where peace does not fade even when other things do not happen or do not last. We are told to live at peace with everyone as much as it depends on us (Romans 12:18), but we know that all of our efforts do not guarantee peaceful relationships. That is why our peace must be found in Christ alone. Even today, we can do much to set our minds upon the peace of Christ, starting with the verse in Ephesians 2.

God, I know that you are the true source of peace which does not depend on any circumstances. Help me set my mind upon you today, trusting in your goodness, and not requiring everything to go the way I want it to.

WHOLEHEARTED COMMITMENT

You must commit yourselves wholeheartedly to these commands that I am giving you today. Repeat them again and again to your children. Talk about them when you are at home and when you are on the road, when you are going to bed and when you are getting up. Tie them to your hands and wear them on your forehead as reminders.

DEUTERONOMY 6:6-8 NLT

God's Word and his commands are structured to be a way of life. They are something that is consistently seen by others in our lives. Coworkers, friends and neighbors, spouses, and children will better understand the importance of God's commands if we give them a place of importance in our daily lives.

Our coworkers will know that we follow Jesus based on our work ethic. Our neighbors will know that we love God based on our speech and the activities we engage in within the neighborhood. Our spouses know that Jesus is the most important thing in our lives because we are quick to forgive. We need to consider what place we have given God's commands in our lives. How we show others today about the importance of Jesus to us matters.

God, I don't ever want there to be any doubt with others that I love you. May I give your commands the highest place of importance in my life so that all may know whom I love and serve.

MADE LIKE US

He had to be made like his brothers in every respect,
so that he might become a merciful and faithful high
priest in the service of God, to make propitiation
for the sins of the people.
HEBREWS 2:17 ESV

Jesus became a man. Every year we remember it, and
as we are growing in God, every year it becomes more
and more incredible. Jesus, the sovereign King of all,
came to earth and was made like us in every respect. He
knows what we feel because he was like us. He walked
in our shoes so he could show us mercy. He is there with
complete understanding when we come to those hard
places in our lives because he is our faithful high priest.

We can stand on his Word and remember that he has
gone before us, for us. He suffered and was made perfect
through it (Hebrews 2:10). Likewise, we will suffer and be
perfected through this path in life. Rejoice, therefore! Each
day is a gift for us to experience the joy of knowing that
Christ came so that we may experience the joy of salvation.

Jesus, as we celebrate the day you gave up everything
to come to earth, remind me again how wonderful it
is to belong to a God who did not consider himself too
important to walk in my shoes. Thank you for the mercy and
love that you extended to me that day, and every day since.

FROM THE HEART

Praise the LORD.
How good it is to sing praises to our God,
how pleasant and fitting to praise him!
PSALM 147:1 NIV

Sometimes a heart doesn't feel like the right place to sing from. With all our daily difficulties and the sadness that sometimes fills our lives, our hearts become heavy and burdened. But sometimes God asks us to sing anyway. And when we do, when we sing for him, our hearts are changed. Suddenly, singing to him is our greatest delight. All else becomes uninteresting. The greatest distraction loses its power, and all we know is his delight in our delight of him.

Trust Jesus, friend. He makes no mistakes, and he knew today's troubles and trials long before we ever lived. His plan is best, and it will be accomplished. Nothing can stop him. Sing therefore because it is good to sing praises to our God. We will delight ourselves in him and sing from the heart, broken or burdened though it may be.

God, thank you that you knew all I would encounter today. Thank you that I can trust you with my day. Thank you that I can give you praise because you are good. Help me sing and delight in you today.

HIS PRIZED CREATION

LORD, how manifold are your works!
In wisdom have you made them all;
the earth is full of your creatures.
Here is the sea, great and wide,
which teems with creatures innumerable,
living things both small and great.
PSALM 104:24-25 ESV

Have you ever thought to yourself, "Surely creation glorifies God so much better than humanity?" It can be genuinely difficult sometimes to see humanity as beautiful. Our lives and hearts show rebellion against a holy God and a love of self at every turn. Do we look out over the glory of a mountain range, knowing the ugliness of our own hearts? Do we wonder if the hills, lakes, trees, and skies know better than we do about how to rejoice in their Maker?

Despite our wicked and wandering hearts, we are the ones God loves. More than the glory of all of his other creations, mankind has captured his heart. Today, let's respond to God. Despite our tendencies to choose other things to worship, he continues to pursue us. Despite the beauty of the natural world, he has chosen us as his prized possession. We worship an awesome God, friend.

Thank you, Lord, that you see me as beautiful and worthy of belonging with you in eternity. May I respond to your kindness to save me; may I worship you alone.

SURRENDERING RIGHTS

What if God, although willing to demonstrate his wrath
and to make his power known, endured with great
patience objects of wrath prepared for destruction? And
he did so to make known the riches of his glory upon
objects of mercy, which he prepared beforehand for glory.

ROMANS 9:22-23 NASB

The cross the Christian bears is to give up all rights and
not become bitter. The Lord gently reminds you of this
whenever your desires start to cloud your vision. He
knows the desires of your heart, but he also knows what
will be good for you. Every act of his toward you is done
out of mercy. You are an object of his mercy, not his wrath
(Romans 9:23), which means that even the things that are
painful or seem harsh are done from a merciful heart and
desire for your welfare. He wants to bless you.

As you move toward a New Year, will you hold tightly
to the things that you consider your rights? Or will you
surrender them to God, trusting his good purposes for
your life and remembering that you are an object of his
mercy. Will you choose to not regret the life that he has
called you to? He is your great reward. Hold tightly to him.

God, forgive me for holding tightly to the things I want
such that I become bitter when you take them away. May I
be always thankful, always rejoicing in your goodness, and
trusting your acts of mercy.

EXTRAORDINARY

As the eyes of slaves
look to the hand of their master,
as the eyes of a female slave
look to the hand of her mistress,
so our eyes look to the LORD our God,
till he shows us his mercy.

PSALM 123:2 NIV

You may be an ordinary person with no particularly special talents but because God has chosen you as his beloved daughter, you now have an extraordinary calling and an extraordinary inheritance. Your life, even in your ordinary days, has an element of extraordinary no matter what the circumstances are because of who you are in Christ. Are you able to see it?

You will too easily miss the amazing things that God adds to your days if your eyes are focused anywhere but on Jesus Christ. You have to be looking to see it. What incredible thing does he want to show you today? Are you too entrenched in this world to notice the wonder-inducing moments in your days? Pray for a mind and a heart that are undistracted so you can witness every extraordinary element that God has planned for you today.

Oh Lord, may your words, your declarations, and your promises not be lost on me today.

IDENTITY IS LOVED

I am convinced that neither death nor life, neither angels nor demons, neither the present nor the future, nor any powers, neither height nor depth, nor anything else in all creation, will be able to separate us from the love of God that is in Christ Jesus our Lord.

ROMANS 8:38-39 NIV

Knowing who you are in Christ and how he perceives you will set you up for success in every area of your life. This is true even on your worst days. Did you offend a friend today? Have you yelled at your children? Did you start an argument just to prove yourself right?

You are deeply loved. You are completely forgiven and fully pleasing to God. You are totally accepted and complete in Christ. You will get to know God in ways you never have known him before. He is continually seeking you out, slow to anger and abounding in mercy, and he longs for you to know how he sees you. When you stumble and fall, his love is constant. Today, walk in confidence of this identity, and let it shape the way you interact with the people around you.

God, I am humbled that even in my messiest moments your love for me does not falter. Teach me to walk in confidence knowing that your love will never be removed from me.

FOCUSED ON FAITHFULNESS

Keep your eyes focused on what is right,
and look straight ahead to what is good.
Be careful what you do,
and always do what is right.
PROVERBS 4:25-26 NCV

You've come to the end of another year. Perhaps it flew by with an intensity you never knew before, or perhaps the days were long and dragged on. However, your year has passed, the Lord walked faithfully with you through it, and he is prepared to do so again. As you look back on your year and prepare for what is to come, remember these things:

- Keep your connections with the Father completely intact,
- Keep your eyes focused on where you are going,
- Understand that you are uniquely made and that is how the Lord will use you the most,
- When you fail—and you will—get up and keep going, setting your eyes on the forgiveness and mercy of God, and
- Surrender your will to Jesus!

God, thank you for your faithfulness to me throughout this year. I have not gone a single day without your love surrounding me. As I walk into the New Year, help me to keep my gaze focused on you and on the things you are calling me to. I love you, Lord!